two at the table

cooking for couples now that the kids are gone

cheryl fall

SASQUATCH BOOKS
SEATTLE

This book is dedicated to my parents,
Nelson and Carmen,
who taught me that cooking together
and bumping buns in the kitchen can be a joy.

Printed in China
Published by Sasquatch Books
Distributed by Publishers Group West
15 14 13 12 11 10 09 08 07   9 8 7 6 5 4 3 2 1

Cover photographs: John A. Rizzo (couple), Cheryl Fall (dishes)
Author photograph: Mary Nevius
Cover & interior design: Kate Basart/Union Pageworks

Library of Congress Cataloging-in-Publication Data is available.

ISBN 1-57061-512-8

SASQUATCH BOOKS
119 South Main Street, Suite 400 | Seattle, WA 98104 | 206.467.4300
www.sasquatchbooks.com | custserv@sasquatchbooks.com

CONTENTS

ACKNOWLEDGMENTS

This book would not exist without the help of my husband, Tony. He patiently endured endless recipe-testing sessions; happily chopped, diced, and grilled; and always gave his advice freely and without worrying about hurting my feelings. Thank you, honey—I love being in the kitchen with you and can hardly wait to start the next book, if you still have the stomach for it.

Thanks also to my children, for inspiring this book in the first place. If they had not gone off to college and started their own lives, I would not have found myself with leftovers out the hooey and the need to change my cooking habits.

I would also like to thank the wonderful folks at Sasquatch Books located in beautiful Seattle, especially my editor, Gary Luke—thank you so much for understanding my vision, stepping out onto a limb, and allowing me to do this project. Working with you is a joy. Also to Rachelle Longé, for her keen eye and sense of humor, and to the rest of the Sasquatch team, especially the production and marketing staffs.

To my agent, Stedman Mays, I would like to extend the warmest of thank yous for sticking by me for over ten years and being the articulate, no-nonsense kind of guy you are, and for making me laugh. Thank you also to Mary Nevius, photographer, mentor, and friend.

PREFACE

This book is for the empty nesters: those of us trying to adjust to planning, buying, and cooking meals for our smaller households. At 76 million strong, there are many of us adjusting to this new phase of life. Incredibly, our generation—those born between 1946 and 1964—are the nation's largest demographic, and as our lifestyles change, so must our daily cooking habits. We've spent at least twenty years cooking family-sized batches of everything from entrées to desserts, which is why I have written this cookbook filled with recipes that feed just two.

Now that there are only two at the table, leftovers seem to appear out of nowhere. This doesn't have to be the case. Cooking for two requires some planning, a new outlook, and some new recipes. While having an empty nest requires major changes in the way we prepare food, it also can yield some fabulous benefits. It leads to a more leisurely lifestyle and, best of all, having time to reconnect with your spouse or life partner. The kitchen can suddenly go from being the hub of the kid-centered home to the most romantic room in the house.

Cooking together and creating new dishes is a wonderful way to connect. Baby boomers are heating up the kitchen and rediscovering both the joys of cooking together and of *being* together.

A WORD ABOUT RECIPE YIELDS

For your convenience and to avoid repetition, all recipes serve two unless otherwise stated.

A WORD ABOUT THE PHOTOGRAPHY

I believe in showing readers the real deal. Therefore, the photos in this book are of the actual finished food, having followed the recipes word for word. Nothing in the photos has been contrived, altered, dummied-up, faked, or otherwise fudged with.

What you see is what you get and it's ready to eat—and in most cases it was gobbled up as soon as the camera powered down.

CHAPTER 1

GETTING TO KNOW
YOU . . . AGAIN

There's a realization that comes over us when we find ourselves with an empty nest. Suddenly the house stays cleaner, and mystery dishes no longer appear in the sink from out of nowhere. Shoes are not there to be tripped over (other than your own), and jackets, backpacks, and schoolbooks are nowhere to be seen. The laundry is neatly folded, and the washer and dryer are actually *empty* for a change. Order has finally been restored.

Satisfied with a now-tidy household, you and your mate find yourself alone. Gone are the shouts, slams, bangs, booms, and other noises of life with kids at home. The kids have flown the coop and moved on. They're away at college or off making independent lives for themselves.

It's finally quiet—almost *too* quiet. You feel a slight pang of separation grief but you realize the quiet is exactly what's supposed to happen. This is what Mother Nature intended. It's time to make some noise for yourselves and do the happy dance!

Shatter that silence and fill the empty air with the sounds of your laughter as you celebrate one of the most important and satisfying stages of your life: your empty nest. When the nest is vacated, it's time to enjoy each other and get a little crazy one on one. It's a little like dating again, and the fun is about to begin.

Your kitchen will now take on a different feel. Gone are the picky eaters and the stragglers expecting meals at all hours of the day. You and your partner now have free rein in the kitchen to cook *what* you want, *when* you want it—and spend quality time together doing it.

The kitchen has always been the heart of your home, and it can become even more important as a way to spend time reconnecting with your mate. By sharing cooking tasks, you can spend time together creating a wonderful meal. You can chop or peel while your mate sautés or grills. I can't think of a better way to get to know each other again than through the joy of cooking.

Cooking for each other—together—is the ultimate expression of love. Pour yourselves a glass of good wine and enjoy your partner to the fullest. Hallelujah! Alone at last!

TURN UP THE HEAT AND GET COOKIN'

Feeling a little rusty in the romance department after twenty to thirty years of child-rearing? Don't worry—your wily, romantic ways will come back to you. Romance is a little like riding a bike: once you've done it, you never forget. To rekindle the romance that's been on hold all this time and get back into a just-the-two-of-us frame of mind, I have several suggestions.

First, consider adding a few aphrodisiacs to your menu. While opinions vary on the effectiveness of sexually stimulating foods, you have to admit that the concept is fun! Science may not be able to prove the effects of stimulating foods because sometimes the best aphrodisiac is the one inside your head—if you believe it, then it's true.

Oysters, asparagus, bananas, celery, figs, ginger, and my personal favorite—chocolate— have been believed for centuries to be aphrodisiacs. Lucky for us, these items are also readily available in just about any grocery store. While thumbing through this book you'll see recipes portioned just for two using these ingredients. Keep these items in stock and you'll always have the tools for a little secret seduction in your pantry.

Second, make a date. You made dates while you were courting, so why not make them again? A note left on the bathroom mirror in the morning hinting at the fun to be had in the kitchen later in the day helps build anticipation. Leaving a voice mail or text message on your honey's phone is another great way to get him or her fired up for the evening's events. Cooking together is fun, and it's a great way to reconnect after a day of work or other activities. As you chop, sauté, and slice, pour two glasses of good wine and chat to catch up on each other's life—and don't forget to flirt.

Third, keep it fun! Who says you have to eat at the table? No one is home to scold you or call you a couple of crazies. Spread a blanket on the floor and serve your meal picnic style, or set up a spot in front of a roaring fire. Turn on some soft, sexy music; light a few candles; and turn on the romance. Be sure to serve oysters or chocolate!

A PANTRY FOR TWO

Admit it. Your pantry is a mess. Go take a peek. It's appalling, isn't it? For years you've had it stuffed with *jumbo* this and *family size* that. Warehouse-sized bags of chips are stale, and there are five boxes of crackers open when you should only use one box at a time. You have entirely too many cans of tomato sauce, chicken soup, and tuna.

You are not alone. My pantry was exactly the same way, and it took some reworking—and rethinking—to get my pantry in order. While cleaning out my pantry, I actually even discovered a few interesting things about myself. What I discovered is that I have a caper fetish (both salt-cured and pickled) and enough jars of roasted red peppers to last until the next ice age. It was no longer necessary to buy in quantity to feed the hoards of young people bopping in and out of the house all the time.

It was just us two now, and my overstocked pantry felt wasteful. I needed to set aside one full day and give it some much-needed love and care. Seriously, it took me a full day, starting at 8:00 in the morning and finally finishing around 5:00 in the afternoon—just in time to start cooking dinner.

I started by making a mental list of everything I used regularly and setting them together on the counter. Next, I took everything else off the pantry shelves and arranged them by food type anywhere there was a flat spot in the kitchen: on the counters, island, table, and spilling out into the family room. (Amazing how stuff accumulates!)

After cleaning the shelves I began pulling items from each pile that were on my list and placing them back in the pantry. There were dozens of items left on the counters that didn't make it back into my reorganized pantry. I boxed these up and took them to a local food bank.

From that time on I was determined to keep my pantry items to a minimum. Everything was clean, organized, and easy to find. What a change!

During the cleanup I also noticed how many store-brand or generic items I had in my pantry—all attempts at saving a few pennies. I saved nothing; I boxed up and hauled out these items. At this point I decided to buy high-quality ingredients rather than cheap imitations. We worked hard raising two children and keeping the household from being ransacked and overrun by youth. It was time we started spoiling ourselves. The pantry is now filled with high-end specialty items: pricey-yet-practical aged balsamic vinegars, fine wines, and special treats.

You will notice that most of the recipes in this book use common ingredients that can be found in any supermarket. These are the items that should, of course, be on your pantry shelves.

There are other items, however, that are not common, such as olive paste or good saffron. These specialty items may need to be tracked down at gourmet markets but are well worth the effort and extra expense—after raising a family, you deserve to spoil yourself with finer ingredients. Enjoy the thrill of the hunt by taking a day with your partner to track down these delectable treasures.

Most of these special gourmet items are worth having simply because they taste divine, but others on the list are far more practical. Take, for example, salted capers. In your normal grocery store, pickled capers are sold in tiny jars, which, once opened, *must* be refrigerated. These tiny jars can take forever to use up, and they begin to grow fur long before we've finished them off. Salted capers, however, are stored in the pantry and will last indefinitely when kept dry. To use them, pull out as many as you need, rinse them in cold water, and they're ready to use. They won't take up fridge space, and they won't grow green hair.

As you review the list of necessary items and clean out your own pantry, pay close attention to the sizes of the items. Now that you are cooking for just the two of you, the large cans of tomato sauce may not always be necessary. Why allow the remainder to go bad in the fridge? Buy the size you really need and waste won't be an issue, which in turn can actually save you money.

What follows is a list of several specialty items that I recommend keeping on hand, and most of them are used at some point in this book. If you have your basic pantry items along with these few simple but unusual items, you'll always have the ingredients for a tasty, healthy gourmet meal for two.

AGED BALSAMIC VINEGAR: Go for one of the good ones from Modena—expensive but worth it. Balsamic vinegar is beautiful in sauces and salad dressings.

ANCHOVY PASTE: Made from ground anchovies and sold in tubes or jars. I always have a 1.6-ounce tube on hand in the refrigerator to flavor sauces and salad dressings. Don't be put off by the anchovy part of the equation. Anchovy paste is a great way to add a salty-yet-savory flavor to many dishes. In fact, you probably consume anchovy paste in restaurant dishes without even knowing it—it's a common ingredient in puttanesca sauce and Caesar salad, among other delicious things.

ARBORIO OR PAELLA RICE: Both of these rice types are small and pearly. Perfect for use in risotto or paella. The stickiness of these types of rice also works well for rice pudding.

ARTICHOKE BOTTOMS: These are just the bottoms of the artichokes and come in a can or jar. Bottoms are meatier than artichoke pieces and are perfect in heartier dishes as well as salads. They can be sliced thinly for an antipasto platter as well. Artichoke hearts can be used interchangeably with bottoms as needed.

BETTER THAN BOUILLON: This is a line of concentrated pastes in beef, chicken, vegetable, and clam flavors. While nothing beats homemade stock, this comes very close and is far superior to bouillon granules and cubes. You can find it in the soup aisle of the grocery store.

CALDO DE TOMATE CON SABOR DE POLLO: A tomato bouillon with a chicken base. This is wonderful as a flavoring for soups, rice, and sauces. You can find it in the Hispanic foods section of most large supermarkets or in Latin markets. It is available in granules or cubes. I prefer the granules as they dissolve more readily than the cubes.

CAPERS: These are the edible buds of an evergreen shrub native to the Mediterranean region. The best ones come from Spain and Italy. Available pickled or preserved in salt. Use them in mustard-based sauces, salad dressings, and pasta salads.

DRIED MUSHROOMS, SUCH AS MORELS OR SHIITAKE: Hydrate dried mushrooms by soaking them in hot water until soft. They are a wonderful addition to hearty meat dishes and soups, and can be kept indefinitely. Keep a variety on hand.

JASMINE RICE: This is a fragrant, long-grain white rice that can be used in place of plain white rice in most recipes. I recommend using a rice steamer rather than boiling for cooking up the lightest, fluffiest grains.

MINCED GARLIC: Available in jars and usually found in the produce section of the supermarket, this is by far one of the most indispensable items to keep in your fridge. There are many recipes in this book calling for minced garlic, and the jarred, refrigerated variety is a perfect substitute for fresh garlic.

OLIVE OIL: I use a lot of olive oil in my cooking. The recipes in this cookbook use extra-virgin olive oil. Be sure to purchase high-quality oils and store them in a cool, dark place, as good oils can go rancid very quickly.

OLIVE PASTE OR TAPENADE: Available fresh or preserved in jars. Great on sandwiches, used in snacks, or in pasta sauces and salad dressings.

PESTO: A sauce made from basil, garlic, pine nuts or walnuts, Parmigiano-Reggiano cheese, salt, and olive oil. Store-bought pesto is not nearly as good as homemade, but a good-quality jar will do in a pinch. Pesto can be used on pasta as well as in salads, soups, or omelets.

PONZU: This is a Japanese, citrus-based marinade and dipping sauce. It's perfect used on chicken (as in Grilled Citrus Chicken Satay, page 80), in salads, and as a marinade. Because it can take a while for two people to use one bottle of ponzu, I have also included a recipe for it (page 80).

SAFFRON: The most expensive spice in the world at up to $55 per quarter ounce. Each saffron thread is the stigma of the saffron flower (*Crocus sativus*) and must be picked by hand. It's well worth spending the extra money on premium saffron as a little goes a long way. Use it to add a beautiful yellow color and an intense flavor and aroma to rice and pasta dishes. I prefer premium Spanish saffron. Don't be fooled by inexpensive saffron, which is nothing more than safflower and is often called Mexican saffron. This imposter does impart a yellow color typical of saffron, but it has no flavor.

SPECIALTY AND FLAVORED OILS: Walnut oil, hazelnut oil, and truffle oil are always in my pantry, as well as flavored oils (usually olive) infused with basil, garlic, tarragon, and other spices. Specialty oils are useful in salad dressings or to dip bread in while snacking.

SPRINKLING SUGAR: Large sugar crystals used for sprinkling on baked goods. I prefer to use crystal white. You can find these larger crystals at stores that carry cake-decorating supplies. (The varieties sold at most grocery stores are made from smaller crystals, and I don't recommend them.) In a pinch, raw sugar crystals can be substituted.

SUN-DRIED TOMATOES IN OLIVE OIL: Keep both whole and julienne strips on hand for ease of preparation. Sun-dried tomatoes are a great substitute for fresh tomatoes in most recipes.

SUN-DRIED TOMATO PASTE: Available in tubes just like anchovy paste. These tubes are great when you only need a tablespoon or two of tomato paste rather than a whole can, and because it is made from sun-dried tomatoes, it has a richer flavor than regular tomato paste.

PACKAGING AND PORTIONING FOR A COUPLE

When talking with other empty nesters, I learned that buying packaged items such as fresh meat or fish is the biggest problem couples face when trimming the kitchen down for two. This is closely followed by bread going stale.

A simple package of premium chicken parts is a prime example. When a person is accustomed to cooking an entire package of chicken, that's exactly what he or she will continue to do. Old habits are hard to break.

Unless you retrain your brain to think differently about portioning and packaging, there are two things that can happen. Either the two of you are going to try to eat all the chicken in one sitting (either because it doesn't make good leftovers or it just feels wasteful not to), or you're going to stick the leftovers in the fridge until you are either sick of eating chicken day after day or it goes bad. Neither scenario is good for you.

There are ways to combat the problem, allowing you not only to package your food for two, but to keep it fresher longer. Get a heat sealer! They are available in the housewares department of any major department store as well as at kitchen supply retailers. I love my

sealer and use it after each trip to the store. I must admit, I still shop at Costco because in my opinion they have the best meat, but of course it's in monster-sized packaging.

The first thing to do when arriving home from shopping is to lay out the fresh meats and breads and get the sealer ready. Open the first package of meat and determine how many pieces you will need per serving.

Remember that what you have often considered a single serving is usually enough for two. With obesity on the rise worldwide, supersizing at home need not be an option. Keep your food and your portions healthy.

A good rule of thumb when bagging and sealing your meat is that a single serving of meat is about the size and thickness of the palm of your hand. That's not much meat, and this means that one rib eye steak per person is entirely too much—one steak can easily serve two people. This is called healthy portioning.

Place the meat in the sealer bags, set the machine to "wet item," and let the machine do its magic as it sucks the air out of the bag and seals the items in a freezer-safe cocoon.

You can use the same technique with breads. I like to split a loaf of bread in two and use one half while it's fresh and freeze the other half. Inevitably though, bread is one of the first things you'll notice going to waste now that you have an empty nest. In this book I have included many recipes to help use up some of the bread that is past its prime. Warning: when bagging and sealing your bread, watch carefully as the machine pulls the air from the bag. Allow the machine to take only as much air as necessary—if it takes too much, the result will be bread that has been sucked flat as a pancake.

Bag and seal all your perishables first and then move on to putting away dry and pantry items to help guard against foodborne illness. Clean your machine well between each food type so that you don't inadvertently find yourself contaminating breads with chicken juices.

My final words of wisdom here: when in doubt, consult your owner's manual.

COOK ONCE, USE TWICE

This is one of my favorite mantras when cooking for just the two of us. A whole chicken is too much food, so I use it twice. The trick is to use it in recipes that are different enough that it won't feel or taste like you are eating leftovers.

For example, prepare Sunday Chicken (page 79) and serve half. Remove the meat from the bones on the other half of the chicken and use this meat on another day in another recipe such as Polenta Verde with Chicken (page 69), Chicken and Vegetable Soup Romano (pages 50–51), or to make a chicken salad.

The same mode of thinking can be applied to meats even *before* they are cooked. A perfect example would be the recipe for Turkey Schnitzel with Mustard Sauce (page 76). Only two cutlets are used in the recipe, but they are sold four to a package. Use your sealer to store and freeze the other two cutlets for another time or another recipe.

You can think along these same lines with certain vegetables as well. For example, purchase a bag of prewashed baby spinach for Spinach and Pear Salad with Strawberry Dressing (page 31). You'll have enough spinach remaining to use in Chickpeas with Chorizo and Spinach (page 53) or in Potato Cake with Egg, Pepper Bacon, and Spinach (page 23) without feeling like you're eating leftovers.

CHAPTER 2

BREAKFAST & LUNCH

country gravy *with* scrambled eggs

french toast bake *with* bananas *and* peanuts

northwest crab omelet

smoked salmon *and* egg panini

veggie lover's crustless quiche

asparagus *with* eggs *and* tomatoes

croque madame frittata

pitas *with* almond cranberry chicken salad

tomato *and* basil omelets *with* red onion *and* provolone

potato cake *with* egg, pepper bacon, *and* spinach

country gravy with
scrambled eggs

This is one of my personal favorite breakfast treats. Because it's heavy on all the things that are not terribly good for us, I limit this treat to once or twice per month, usually on a lazy Saturday morning, but I would eat it every day if given the chance. Traditionally this gravy is served over fluffy, homemade biscuits, but it is just as tasty over toast or croissants. Any leftovers can be reheated in the microwave the next morning.

¼ pound pork breakfast sausage (about 4 links)
1 tablespoon all-purpose flour
1 cup milk
4 large eggs
1 tablespoon water
1 tablespoon butter
Salt and pepper
2 tablespoons fresh chopped parsley

1. Heat a large skillet over medium heat. Remove the sausage from the skins (unnecessary if using bulk sausage) and put in the skillet. Brown the sausage, stirring constantly, about 10 minutes. Remove as much of the sausage from the pan as possible, reserving the drippings.

2. Add the flour to the drippings and stir to form a paste. Add the milk and stir constantly until the mixture begins to thicken. Add the sausage back to the pan and stir. Remove from the heat and keep the gravy warm while preparing the eggs.

3. Whisk the eggs and water together in a bowl. In a clean skillet, melt the butter over medium heat. Add the eggs and scramble. Season to taste with salt and pepper.

4. Serve the eggs and gravy over your favorite biscuits or bread, and sprinkle with the parsley.

french toast bake with bananas and peanuts

It's my belief that a married couple should never stop flirting or courting. I recommend starting your flirt in the morning and carrying on throughout the rest of the day. You can begin flirting across the table from each other while enjoying this bread-pudding-style breakfast. This is a terrific use for leftover bread such as brioche or challah and it's perfect for a Sunday morning breakfast in bed. Or serve it on a lazy Saturday morning in the kitchen with plenty of piping-hot coffee. It also makes a nice dessert.

> One 14-ounce can sweetened condensed milk (not evaporated milk)
> 4 eggs, beaten
> 1 teaspoon rum or rum extract
> ½ teaspoon pure vanilla extract
> 2 to 3 slices of bread, cubed (about 2 cups)
> 1 large banana, sliced
> ½ cup peanuts
> Maple syrup

1. Preheat the oven to 425°F. Butter a casserole dish; set aside.

2. In a large bowl beat together the condensed milk and the eggs. Add the rum extract, vanilla, and the bread cubes. Stir gently to combine without crushing the bread cubes.

3. Pour the mixture into the buttered casserole dish. Bake for 20 minutes, or until golden brown.

4. To serve, place a mound of the bread pudding on a plate and top with the banana, peanuts, and maple syrup.

northwest crab omelet

SERVES 1

I love the sound of pans clanging in the kitchen on a weekend morning because there's a good chance this omelet is being made and served on a tray in grand style. Oh, the delights of breakfast in bed! Flowers, coffee, juice, and omelets for two. If you're serving up this treat to your hubby instead of him serving it to you, don't forget the flowers—guys dig them on their bed tray too. If you don't have fresh crab, you can substitute canned crab. This omelet also makes a delightful lunch or light supper. I've given the directions here on a per-omelet basis—make as many as you need, or just one to share.

2 eggs
1 teaspoon water
Salt and pepper
1 tablespoon butter
¼ cup fresh crab, shelled and picked through
¼ ripe avocado, thinly sliced
1 tablespoon chopped red onion
2 tablespoons sour cream

1. In a small bowl beat the eggs with the water. Season to taste with salt and pepper. Heat the butter in a medium nonstick skillet over medium-high heat. Add the egg mixture, scraping the bottom of the pan and swirling until the eggs begin to set.

2. When the eggs are almost set, arrange the crab, avocado, onions, and sour cream on the omelet, placing the items to one side (not along the center), and fold. Serve immediately.

smoked salmon and egg panini

These panini (grilled Italian sandwiches) are the ideal packable treat for the couple on the go and are equally tasty for breakfast, lunch, or a light supper. While they're easy and quick to make, you can shorten your last-minute prep time by cooking the scrambled eggs the night before or while the panini grill heats up. Simply assemble and cook the sandwiches before the two of you head out the door on your next adventure. I've used smoked salmon, but smoked trout or steelhead is also fabulous in this sandwich. In a pinch, smoked ham or turkey will suffice as well, but the smoked salmon definitely lends an air of luxury to this take-and-go meal. If you have any leftover green vegetables, tuck them into the bread before grilling for added flavor.

2 kaiser-style fresh bakery rolls
2 tablespoons cream cheese, softened
½ cup shredded smoked salmon
2 eggs, scrambled
1 thin slice red onion
2 slices deli Havarti cheese
Olive oil cooking spray

tip

Electric panini grills give the sandwiches their distinctive grill marks; they are available in most kitchen stores. If you don't have a panini grill, any nonstick grill pan will work just as well. Place a weighted plate atop the sandwiches to flatten them after putting them in the grill pan.

1. Preheat your panini grill to medium heat.

2. Cut each roll in half. Smooth one tablespoon of the cream cheese on one side of each roll. Top the cream cheese with half of the salmon and half of the eggs. Separate the red onion slice into rings and arrange half of the rings on each roll atop the eggs. Place a slice of Havarti on the fillings and then top with the other side of the roll, pressing slightly to keep the filling from tumbling out.

3. Lightly spray the top of each sandwich with the cooking spray and place the sandwiches in the grill. Cook for 2 to 3 minutes, or until the bread is golden brown and the cheese is melted. Serve the panini at room temperature.

veggie lover's crustless quiche

Quiche without a crust? Why not! Eliminating the crust saves both time and calories. If you prefer a crust, you can use your favorite pie crust recipe or a frozen pie shell, but since my hubby and I tend to scoop out the filling and leave the shell behind, we eliminated it altogether. This recipe is suitable for more than just breakfast or brunch. We like to take this along on long romantic drives and leisurely picnics, because it's just as tasty at room temperature as it is hot from the oven.

4 large eggs
¾ cup half-and-half
½ cup crushed saltine crackers
½ teaspoon baking powder
3 teaspoons butter
½ cup diced carrots
½ cup peeled, sliced zucchini or yellow squash
½ cup green beans
¼ cup chopped red or green bell pepper
¼ cup chopped onion
Salt and pepper

1. Preheat the oven to 425°F. Butter a 9- by 9-inch square pan; set aside.

2. In a large bowl beat the eggs with the half-and-half. Add the crackers and the baking powder and stir well to combine.

3. In a small skillet, melt the butter over medium-high heat. Add the vegetables and onions and sauté until the onions are transparent, about 5 minutes. Add the vegetable mixture to the egg mixture and stir to combine. Season to taste with salt and pepper.

4. Pour the quiche mixture into the buttered pan. Bake for 25 minutes, or until golden brown and slightly puffed. Cut into squares and serve hot or at room temperature.

asparagus with
eggs and tomatoes

*T**his recipe is quick, simple, and delicious, especially on a cold morning. It also makes a lovely supper on a busy evening when there's not much time to cook. It's made with just a few basic ingredients—it's almost too easy. Frozen asparagus can be used instead if fresh asparagus is not in season. Zucchini and eggplant are also fabulous substitutes. This recipe can easily be adapted for a crowd if you're hosting a brunch. This dish is best served in shallow bowls with plenty of crusty bread to sop up the juices. A great use for the remaining ¾ cup of diced tomatoes is Chicken and Vegetable Soup Romano (pages 50–51).*

1 bunch (about 12 spears) of asparagus, trimmed
¾ cup (half a 14.5-ounce can) diced tomatoes in juice
2 cloves garlic, minced
¼ cup dry white wine
Salt and freshly ground black pepper
2 large eggs at room temperature

> ## tip
> Using a baking sheet under the casserole dish makes it easier to move the hot casserole dish in and out of the oven.

1. Preheat the oven to 425°F.

2. Cut the trimmed asparagus into 1-inch pieces and place in a shallow casserole dish. Combine the tomatoes, garlic, and wine in a small bowl. Season to taste with salt and pepper. Pour the tomato mixture over the asparagus.

3. Place the filled casserole on a baking sheet and bake for 20 minutes, or until the asparagus is tender and the juices are bubbling. Remove the casserole from the oven and crack the two eggs over the casserole. Put the casserole back in the oven for 5 to 10 minutes, or until the egg whites are just set. Serve immediately.

croque madame frittata

*A*nything French is romantic and sure to elicit a wink or two from across the room. Croque Madame is a famous French sandwich, similar to a grilled cheese but with the addition of a slice of ham and a fried egg. In this recipe I've combined the classic ingredients in a different way, creating a frittata for two. It's perfect for brunch or breakfast on the terrace.

> 4 large eggs
> 2 tablespoons butter
> 1 tablespoon all-purpose flour
> 1 cup milk
> ½ cup grated Gruyère cheese
> Salt and pepper
> ½ cup cubed cooked ham
> 2 slices white or whole wheat bread, cubed

1. Preheat the oven to 425°F. Butter a 9-inch pie pan; set aside.

2. Beat the eggs in a large bowl. In a medium skillet, melt the butter over medium-high heat. Stir in the flour to form a paste. Add the milk, whisking constantly until the mixture thickens, about 5 minutes. Stir in the Gruyère. Season to taste with salt and pepper.

3. Add the cheese mixture to the eggs a little at a time, whisking constantly. Add the ham and bread cubes, stirring gently just to combine the ingredients.

4. Pour the mixture into the buttered pan. Bake for 15 to 20 minutes, or until set. Cut into wedges to serve.

pitas with almond cranberry chicken salad

If you have any chicken left over, this is the place to use it. The cranberries add a sweet-and-sour touch to this salad, while the almonds add some crunch. You can serve the salad in purchased pita bread pockets, but it's even better served on homemade Rustic Flatbread (pages 182–83), folded taco style. This recipe makes just enough for two, so you don't need to worry about your chicken salad separating while languishing in the fridge, waiting to be finished up.

1½ cups diced, cooked chicken
¼ cup diced celery
¼ cup chopped dried cranberries
¼ cup sliced, toasted almonds
⅓ cup mayonnaise
1 tablespoon cider vinegar
½ teaspoon sugar
¼ cup finely diced red onion
Salt and pepper

1. In a medium bowl combine the chicken, celery, cranberries, and almonds.

2. In a separate bowl combine the remaining ingredients to make a dressing and season to taste with salt and pepper. Add the dressing to the chicken mixture and stir to combine. Serve in pita bread pockets.

tomato and basil omelets with
red onion and provolone

We were testing this recipe while our oldest daughter was home from college for the weekend, just after the fall semester had started. I had a basket of fresh Roma tomatoes that my neighbor had picked from his own bountiful garden and had brought over the day before. I thought it would be nice to add them to my omelet recipe, which at that point was sans veggies. I asked my daughter if she would be the official taste tester for the day, and luckily she had no other plans. Her reaction to this omelet was "Oooh, ummmm, this tastes so fresh!" 'Nuff said—the recipe was ready!

3 slices deli provolone
2 Roma tomatoes
4 large eggs at room temperature*
1 tablespoon water
Salt and pepper
Nonstick cooking spray
2 slices red onion
4 tablespoons fresh chopped basil or ready-made pesto**

1. Cut each slice of provolone in half and cut each tomato into five slices.

2. Whisk the eggs with the water in a small bowl. Season to taste with salt and pepper.

3. Heat a small nonstick skillet over high heat. When nice and hot (test it with a bead of water—if the water skips and sizzles, the pan is ready), coat the pan with the nonstick cooking spray. Pour in half of the egg mixture and cook until firm, swirling the pan and scraping the bottom to distribute and cook the egg mixture evenly.

4. When the mixture begins to firm up, layer three half-slices of the provolone on one half of the omelet (the other half will be folded over the filling) and top with half of the red onion slices and five of the tomato slices. Sprinkle 2 tablespoons of the basil over the filling and fold the omelet. Slide the finished omelet onto a plate and repeat for the second omelet.

* *Eggs at room temperature won't stick to the pan as much as chilled eggs.*

** *I always keep a jar of good-quality, ready-made pesto in my pantry. It's perfect for recipes requiring smaller quantities, and the open jar will keep well in the refrigerator for a good week. Use the remainder in salad dressings or tossed with hot, cooked pasta!*

potato cake with egg, pepper bacon, and spinach

This omelet is reminiscent of a Spanish tortilla de patata *but with a preparation shortcut to beat all shortcuts—using fresh, prepackaged hash brown potatoes. Of course, you can also use freshly grated potatoes. This dish is delightfully romantic when paired with glasses of chilled champagne or mimosas.*

2 tablespoons olive oil, divided
2 cups fresh packaged hash brown potatoes, O'Brien style
3 eggs, beaten
3 slices pepper bacon, fried crispy and crumbled
1 cup frozen spinach, drained

1. Heat one tablespoon of the oil in a large nonstick skillet over medium-high heat.

2. Combine the remaining ingredients and mix well. Pour the mixture into the skillet and press with the back of a spatula to even out the surface. Turn the heat to medium-low and cook for 8 to 10 minutes, or until the center begins to set.

3. Invert a plate over the pan and carefully turn the omelet onto the plate. Heat the remaining olive oil in the pan. Return the omelet to the pan, cooked side up, by sliding the omelet from the plate into the pan. Cook the other side for 5 to 8 minutes, or until the entire omelet is set. Serve warm.

CHAPTER 3

SNACKS, STARTERS & SALADS

asian summer salad

intermezzo pasta salad

broad beans in vinaigrette

jazzy sweet-*and*-sour cabbage salad

antipasto for two

spinach *and* pear salad *with* strawberry dressing

apple, pine nut, *and* broccoli salad

parmesan tomato crostini

toast crisps *with* herbed goat cheese spread

warm eggplant dip *with* pita bread

lemony fruit cups

balsamic lentil salad

cucumber salad *with* yogurt mint dressing

stuffed mushrooms *with* fresh parsley

stubby oven fries *with* easy garlic alioli

asian summer salad

Chilled noodles and crispy raw vegetables combined with a slightly sweet vinaigrette make this salad refreshingly perfect for a hot summer evening. The somen noodles used in this recipe are very fine, thin noodles and can be found in the Asian section of every large grocery store. They are packaged in bundles of five, making proportioning the noodles very easy—use one bundle per person. Because the noodles cook quickly and need to be immediately cooled in running water, enlist the help of your partner, who can chop the vegetables and mix the dressing while you mind the noodles. Two in the kitchen is so much more fun than one!

2 bundles tomoshiraga somen noodles
¼ cup rice vinegar
2 tablespoons sesame oil
1 tablespoon granulated sugar
¼ teaspoon salt
1 tablespoon black sesame seeds*
¼ cup seeded, chopped red bell pepper
¼ cup shelled edamame**
½ cup peeled, seeded, and chopped cucumber
1 green onion, thinly sliced

1. In a medium saucepan, bring 4 cups of water to a boil. Add the somen noodles and cook until tender, about 4 minutes. Watch them—they cook quickly! Put the noodles in a colander, run cold water over them to cool them and prevent any further cooking, and drain.

2. Combine the vinegar, oil, sugar, salt, and sesame seeds to make the dressing. Pour the dressing over the noodles. Top with the bell pepper, edamame, cucumber, and green onion. Serve immediately.

*   Black sesame seeds are available at Asian markets and specialty food stores. White or toasted sesame seeds may be substituted as needed.

** You can use fresh or frozen edamame. If frozen, allow them to thaw before combining dressing ingredients.

intermezzo pasta salad

*T*he beautiful color of the fresh vegetables combined with the pasta and balsamic vinaigrette makes this salad the perfect opening act for a lingering romantic candlelit dinner or a light lunch. You can use acini di pepe, orzo, or other very small pasta for this salad—even couscous. Do use good balsamic vinegar for this recipe. Now that it's just the two of you, splurging on finer ingredients isn't just worth it—it's essential for putting a little life back in your cooking after all these years.

FOR THE SALAD:

½ cup acini di pepe
¼ teaspoon salt
1 cup peeled, seeded, and diced cucumber
¼ cup seeded and chopped yellow bell pepper
½ cup cherry or grape tomatoes, quartered
1 cup fresh chopped baby spinach
2 green onions, sliced
¼ cup crumbled feta cheese
¼ cup halved, pitted kalamata olives

FOR THE DRESSING:

¼ cup extra-virgin olive oil
2 tablespoons balsamic vinegar
1 clove garlic, minced
Salt and pepper

> ## tip
> Go easy on the salt! The feta cheese and kalamata olives contain more than enough salt for this dish.

1. Cook the pasta in rapidly boiling water with the salt. Rinse the pasta with cool water and drain. Toss the pasta with the remaining salad ingredients.

2. To make the dressing, place all ingredients in a jar with a tight-fitting lid and shake well to blend. Pour the dressing over the salad and toss to coat. Chill the salad at least one hour before serving to allow the flavors to develop.

broad beans in vinaigrette

SERVES 2 AS A SALAD OR 4 AS AN APPETIZER

*T*his is one of those recipes that you can prepare in the morning and let sit in the refrigerator during the day allowing you to spend some of that much-needed quality time with your sweetie. In this recipe I like to use large Spanish dried broad beans, known as Judios Blancos or Judión beans, but any large dried broad bean will do, including fava beans, white kidney beans, and extra-large lima beans. If you prefer a smaller bean, Great Northern beans—my husband's favorite—are also a good substitute. Also, be sure to use good-quality olive oil and white wine vinegar for this recipe for the best flavor.

½ cup dried (about 2 cups cooked) *Judios Blancos** or white kidney beans
1 bay leaf, fresh or dried
¼ cup finely chopped onion
2 cloves garlic, minced
½ cup chopped bell pepper**
¼ cup chopped celery
½ cup white wine vinegar
¼ cup extra-virgin olive oil
¼ teaspoon dried oregano
¼ teaspoon red pepper flakes
Salt and freshly ground black pepper

1. Soak the beans in a large bowl of water for at least 8 hours or overnight. Do not drain the soaking liquid.

2. Transfer the beans and the soaking liquid to a medium saucepan. Add water to fully cover the beans, with one or two inches of additional water and add the bay leaf. Bring to a boil. Turn down the heat to a simmer and cook until the beans are tender, about 1½ to 2 hours. (Remember: older beans than have been sitting in the pantry for a while take longer to cook than recently purchased beans.)

3. Drain the beans and let them cool to room temperature. Discard the bay leaf.

4. In a small bowl, combine the remaining ingredients except the salt and pepper. Pour the mixture over the beans and allow them to marinate in the refrigerator at least 2 hours. Season to taste with salt and pepper. Serve chilled.

*   Judios Blancos *can be ordered from specialty or Spanish food markets. If you don't have any dried beans on hand, a 15-ounce can of salt-free cannellini (white kidney) beans, rinsed and drained, makes an excellent substitute.*

**   *I use a combination of red and green bell peppers for extra color.*

jazzy sweet-and- sour cabbage salad

Across between a salad and a slaw, this yummy dish is wonderful with roasted or barbecued meats, and tastes even better the second day. For a change of pace, substitute red cabbage. If you have a romantic weekend getaway coming up, this salad packs well and is perfect for a picnic for two.

> 2 cups shredded napa cabbage
> 1 tart apple, such as Granny Smith, peeled, cored, and diced
> ¼ cup chopped green onions
> ½ cup dried cranberries
> 1 tablespoon canola oil
> 2 tablespoons seasoned rice vinegar
> ½ teaspoon soy sauce

1.   In a medium bowl, toss together the cabbage, apple, green onions, and cranberries.

2.   Place the remaining ingredients in a jar with a tight-fitting lid. Shake well to combine the ingredients and create the dressing. Pour the dressing over the salad and chill for one hour before serving.

antipasto for two

An antipasto platter can be prepared earlier in the day and brought out when the time is right for a relaxing bite with your lifelong pal. There are as many versions of an antipasto platter as there are cooks, and there is no right or wrong version, so feel free to personalize it to your own tastes. However, most Italian cooks agree that it should contain at least two each of the following: cured meats, cheeses, pickled vegetables, and olives. Fresh fruits in season or dried fruits are also a nice addition. Serve the antipasti with a good, crusty bread or grissini (crispy breadsticks). Use the list below to help you assemble your own perfect antipasto misto (mixed antipasto) platter. Because of the infinite variety of antipasto items, this is by no means a complete list.

MEATS: Prosciutto, Genoa salami, speck, coppa (sweet or hot), mortadella, good-quality anchovy fillets (rinsed), hard-boiled eggs, sardines, bonito in olive oil, copacola

CHEESES: Feta, Asiago, fontina, provolone, shaved Parmigiano-Reggiano, Gorgonzola, mozzarella

VEGETABLES: Sun-ripened tomatoes, sliced cucumber, fresh green beans, fresh fava or broad beans, celery stalks, green onions, cold grilled zucchini or other squash, fresh or marinated mushrooms, capers, marinated eggplant and artichoke hearts, roasted red peppers, small cornichons (dill pickles), marinated red onions, peperoncini (pickled yellow peppers), pickled cherry peppers, giardiniera (pickled vegetable salad), thinly sliced red onion, stuffed grape leaves

OLIVES AND SPREADS: Kalamata olives, marinated olive blends, country olive mix, stuffed olives, green olives, ripe olives, caponata (a tomato and eggplant spread), olive tapenade

FRUITS: Melons of any variety but especially honeydew and cantaloupe, figs (fresh or dried), pears, plums, sweet cherry tomatoes, dried apricots

DRESSINGS: Italian dressing (bottled) or garlicky alioli, served on the side

tip

By keeping jars of marinated vegetables and olives in your pantry and an assortment of cheeses and deli meats in your refrigerator, you can put together an antipasto platter quickly for unexpected guests, create a small antipasto platter as an appetizer, or arrange a larger one for a nice, light lunch.

spinach and pear salad
with strawberry dressing

This is such an elegant, pretty salad. I like to make this during the autumn months or for a nice Sunday dinner. There's no need to keep a half-dozen bottles of half-used salad dressings in the fridge either. With a few simple ingredients—in this case, oil, vinegar, and fruit jams—you can quickly and easily create your own fresh dressings in a variety of flavors. Here I have used strawberry, but other jams are great as well. Try it with raspberry, apricot, peach, or blueberry!

    2 cups fresh baby spinach leaves, washed and dried
    1 ripe pear, such as Bartlett, Bosc, Comice, or Anjou
    ½ cup crumbled feta cheese
    ¼ cup walnuts
    2 tablespoons walnut oil*
    1 tablespoon cider vinegar
    2 tablespoons strawberry jam
    ¼ teaspoon salt

1. Arrange one cup of spinach on each of two salad plates. Cut the pear in half lengthwise and remove the core. Cut each pear half into thin slices and arrange on the beds of spinach. Sprinkle half the feta and walnuts over each salad.

2. To make the dressing, combine the remaining ingredients in a jar with a tight-fitting lid. Shake vigorously to combine the ingredients. Pour the dressing over the salads and enjoy.

* *Other nut oils, such as hazelnut, will work as well. Plain canola oil is another good choice for this salad, but don't use olive oil here—the flavor is too strong with fruit.*

apple, pine nut, and broccoli salad

This is a crisp, tasty salad with apples at its core (pun intended). Apples are delightfully romantic—the ancient Greeks revered the apple as a potent aphrodisiac. So potent were its purported powers that all a man had to do was toss an apple to his intended; if she caught it, a wedding was imminent. While this salad is wonderful fresh, it's even better the next day after the flavors have a chance to meld. Be sure to use firm, tart apples and don't peel the fruit—apples store most of their nutrients directly under the skin, plus there's a lot of good fiber hiding in it.

> 1 large Granny Smith, Jonathan, or Rome Beauty apple
> ¼ cup pine nuts, toasted*
> 1 cup chopped broccoli
> ¼ cup chopped celery
> 1 tablespoon chopped red onion
> ¼ cup mayonnaise
> 2 tablespoons apple cider vinegar
> 1 teaspoon sugar

1. Core the apple and cut it into ¼-inch cubes. Place the apple, pine nuts, broccoli, and celery in a medium bowl.

2. Combine the remaining ingredients in a small bowl to make the dressing. Pour the dressing over the apple mixture and toss to blend.

* *Pine nuts can go rancid very quickly. To prevent spoilage, store unused pine nuts tightly wrapped in the freezer or buy them in smaller quantities in the bulk foods department. Toast pine nuts by heating a small skillet over medium-high heat. Add the pine nuts and toast, turning often. Be careful—they can burn very quickly.*

parmesan tomato crostini

Crostini are so easy to make and even easier to eat. They're one of our favorite snack foods after a day of running errands. Delicious and attractive to behold, they're terrific for impromptu gatherings with friends as well. Now that it's just the two of us and we do what we want when we want, we've been known to have crostini and wine for a light meal on a busy day. It's a bit like having an adult pizza.

FOR THE CROSTINI:

Four ½-inch-thick slices of crusty bread
1 ripe Roma tomato, thinly sliced
¼ cup freshly grated Parmesan cheese

FOR THE DRESSING:

1 teaspoon red wine vinegar
1 clove garlic, minced
¼ teaspoon salt
¼ teaspoon freshly ground black pepper
¼ teaspoon dried basil, crushed

tip

If you have fresh basil available, use one leaf per toast. This is also a fun recipe for experimentation: try using fresh sage, rosemary, or oregano on your crostini.

1. Preheat the oven to 400°F. Put the bread on a baking sheet and toast in the oven for about 2 minutes, or until golden brown (watch them so they don't burn).

2. Top each piece of toast with ¼ of the tomato slices and the Parmesan.

3. Mix the dressing ingredients together in a small bowl. Drizzle the dressing over the crostini and serve immediately.

toast crisps with
herbed goat cheese spread

MAKES ABOUT ¾ CUP OF SPREAD

*S*ometimes the simplest recipes can be the best. This recipe goes together fast and is perfect for an afternoon snack. Fresh goat cheese, combined with simple herbs and minced garlic, creates a tasty spread for
homemade toast crisps. One of the things we have noticed in our home is that loaves of bread go to waste
with just two of us there to eat them. This recipe is useful for using up that bread and is perfect for day-old
or slightly stale bread. I used an assortment of breads here for "show," but even plain old white bread will
work beautifully.

FOR THE TOAST CRISPS:

    3 or 4 slices of bread
    Olive oil cooking spray

FOR THE SPREAD:

    One 5.5-ounce log fresh goat cheese, at room temperature
    1 teaspoon minced garlic
    1 teaspoon herbes de Provence

1. Preheat the oven to 350°F.

2. Trim the crusts from the bread and cut each slice of bread into 4 or 6 pieces. Place a
   baking rack on a baking sheet. Arrange the bread pieces on the rack and spray lightly
   with the cooking spray. Turn the pieces over and spray the other sides. Bake the bread
   pieces for 3 to 5 minutes, or until crispy and lightly browned.

3. To make the spread, in a small bowl combine all of the ingredients. Serve at room
   temperature on the toast crisps.

warm eggplant dip with pita bread

MAKES 1½ CUPS OF DIP

In Europe around 400 years ago, eggplant was known as the "apple of love" and was considered a potent aphrodisiac. This was due to eggplant's high potassium content, which provides extra energy and increases hormone levels—just in case you're pulling a romantic all-nighter. Eggplant can be bitter, but knowing how to choose the right one can lessen your chances of bringing home one that will bite. Look for eggplants with smooth, very firm skin—leave the ones with soft skin or mushy spots where they are. I have also found that the lighter the eggplant's color, the milder the flesh.

This recipe is a family reunion of sorts: the eggplant is joined by its cousins the tomato and the green pepper—all deliciously nonlethal members of the otherwise poisonous nightshade family. The dip is best served warm; it may be served with ready-made pita bread but is even better with Rustic Flatbread (pages 182–83).

> 1 medium globe eggplant*
> 3 tablespoons olive oil, divided
> 1 medium onion, diced
> 2 cloves garlic, minced
> ¼ cup diced green bell pepper
> 2 large Roma tomatoes, seeded and diced
> ½ teaspoon salt
> ½ teaspoon freshly ground black pepper
> ¼ cup dry white wine
> 1 teaspoon curry powder

1. Preheat the oven to 400°F.

2. Slice the eggplant in half lengthwise and brush the flesh with 1 tablespoon of the olive oil. Place the eggplant sections flesh-side-down on a baking sheet. Roast the eggplant for 15 minutes, or until the flesh is tender.

3. Let the eggplant cool for several minutes, or until you can handle it without burning your hands. Remove the skin from the eggplant in sections—it will separate from the flesh easily once it has been roasted—and dice the eggplant flesh.

4. Heat the remaining olive oil in a large skillet. Add the onions and sauté until transparent, about 5 minutes. Add the garlic, bell pepper, and tomatoes and sauté until the tomatoes begin to soften, about 5 minutes. Add the eggplant, salt and pepper, wine, and curry powder. Cook until half of the liquid has been absorbed and the mixture has slightly thickened, about 10 minutes.

5. Spoon the dip into a pretty bowl and serve warm with pita bread.

* *There are two types of eggplant commonly available in most grocery stores: large, round purple globe and the skinnier, lighter-skinned Japanese variety. For this recipe, use the former.*

lemony fruit cups

Fruit salad *is a nice alternative to a green salad with lunch or dinner and also makes a terrific light breakfast or dessert, especially during warmer weather. You can customize it to your own tastes: use peaches and plums in summer and apples and pears in the fall. Just remember: the trick to the best fruit salad is the freshness of the fruits. The lemon juice will keep the fruit from discoloring and adds a nice tangy flavor. Serve the salad in pretty cups or use hollowed-out orange halves for an extra-nice touch.*

1 cup cubed honeydew melon
1 orange, peeled and sectioned
1 medium papaya, peeled and cut into ½-inch chunks
1 banana, sliced into ½-inch rounds
2 kiwifruit, peeled and quartered
1 fresh lemon
½ tablespoon granulated sugar

In a medium bowl combine all the fruit except the lemon. Wash the lemon and add ½ teaspoon of its zest to the fruit. Cut the lemon in half and remove the seeds. Squeeze the juice over the fruit. Sprinkle the sugar over the fruit mixture and toss gently to coat.

balsamic lentil salad

This legume is one of our favorite pantry items and is very popular in the Near East and Africa, as well as in India and parts of Europe. The versatility of lentils is the key to their popularity, as they can be made into delicious salads like this one, served in savory dishes, or added to soup and stews. Lentils also cook quickly, making them ideal for quick-fix weeknight meals. Older boomers may remember eating lentils often as children, because during World War II, Americans were encouraged to eat lentils as part of the wartime rationing. Lentils caught on, and their use continued well after the war. Interestingly, a full third of the lentils consumed in the United States are grown in the Palouse region of Washington and northern Idaho.

¼ cup dried brown lentils
2 tablespoons olive oil, divided
¼ cup chopped onion
¼ cup chopped celery with leafy tops
¼ cup thinly sliced carrots
1 clove garlic, minced
¼ teaspoon salt
¼ teaspoon freshly ground black pepper
1 small bay leaf
2 tablespoons good-quality balsamic vinegar
½ teaspoon fresh or ¼ teaspoon dried thyme
1 tablespoon fresh or ½ teaspoon dried parsley

1. Rinse and pick through the lentils, getting rid of any dirt or debris that may be lurking.

2. In a medium saucepan, heat 1 tablespoon of the olive oil over medium heat. Add the onions and celery and cook until the onions are transparent, about 5 minutes. Add the lentils, carrots, garlic, salt, and pepper. Add water to cover the mixture by 1 inch and drop in the bay leaf. Bring to a boil and reduce the heat to a simmer. Cook uncovered for 20 minutes, or until the lentils are tender. Do not overcook, as you don't want the lentils to be mushy.

3. When the lentils are cooked, remove the bay leaf and drain off any excess liquid. Allow the lentils to cool.

4. While the lentils are cooling, mix the remaining olive oil with the balsamic vinegar, thyme, and parsley in a small bowl to make the dressing. Pour the dressing over the cooled lentils, toss to coat, and serve.

cucumber salad with
yogurt mint dressing

This is a refreshing salad that packs well for picnics and getaways for two, and it features a tasty, versatile dressing. Try the dressing tossed with cooked, cooled potato cubes instead of cucumber for a fresh take on potato salad, or serve the dressing as a dip with freshly made Rustic Flatbread (pages 182–83). We have even been known to take the flatbread hot off the griddle, fill it with this salad, and get giddy.

1 medium cucumber, peeled and diced
1 cup plain yogurt
1 tablespoon olive oil
1 clove garlic, minced
1 teaspoon granulated sugar
¼ teaspoon salt
¼ teaspoon freshly ground black pepper
2 to 3 tablespoons fresh, chopped mint leaves

Place the cucumber in a small bowl. In a separate bowl, combine the remaining ingredients and pour over the cucumber—you may not use all the dressing, depending on the size of the cucumber. Refrigerate any remaining dressing until ready to use.

stuffed mushrooms with fresh parsley

*M*ost recipes for stuffed mushrooms make enough of them to feed a small army. I like to make just enough for the two of us to enjoy on a Friday evening with a nice glass of wine as we prepare the rest of our evening meal. This recipe uses anchovy paste, but these mushrooms do not taste fishy—instead, it serves up a savory, salty flavoring. Once you rethink it, you'll find yourself using anchovy paste often.

4 to 7 medium white mushrooms
2 tablespoons butter, softened
1 teaspoon anchovy paste
2 tablespoons plain dry bread crumbs
1 tablespoon finely minced onion
1 tablespoon dry white wine
2 tablespoons chopped fresh parsley, divided

1. Preheat the oven to 350°F.

2. Clean the mushrooms by gently wiping off any dirt with a clean towel (never clean mushrooms in water—it ruins them). Remove the stems from the mushrooms and place the caps facedown on a baking sheet. Cut off the dry ends of the mushroom stems and discard. Finely chop the remaining parts of the stems and reserve.

3. To make the filling, in a small bowl combine the butter, anchovy paste, bread crumbs, onions, wine, 1 tablespoon of the chopped parsley, and the reserved mushroom stems. Spoon the filling equally into each mushroom cap, mounding the mixture slightly on the tops. Bake the stuffed mushroom caps for 10 to 12 minutes or until the tops are lightly browned.

4. Place the stuffed mushrooms on a serving plate, sprinkle the remaining parsley over them, and serve.

stubby oven fries with easy garlic alioli

By cutting out the frying process and baking these fries instead, you'll immediately lighten them up—which is great because the garlic alioli will bring them back into the junk food range of fat content. This is OK with us because we love 'em, especially when we're watching movies on a lazy evening at home. I call them "stubby" because I prefer to use smaller potatoes when making oven fries. I find that when the wedges are smaller and stubbier, they cook more evenly, and I don't have fries with soggy centers. The garlic alioli is quick and easy, and makes just enough for two.

FOR THE FRIES:

>   2 to 3 small russet potatoes
>   2 tablespoons olive oil
>   ¼ teaspoon granulated garlic
>   Salt and freshly ground black pepper

FOR THE GARLIC ALIOLI:

>   2 tablespoons mayonnaise
>   1 clove garlic, minced
>   ¼ teaspoon dried parsley flakes

1. Preheat the oven to 425°F.

2. Cut each potato lengthwise into wedges about ½ inch thick. In a bowl, toss the potato wedges with the olive oil, granulated garlic, and salt and pepper to taste, coating each potato wedge thoroughly.

3. Arrange the potatoes in a single layer on a baking sheet. Bake the potato wedges for 15 to 20 minutes, or until cooked through and golden brown.

4. Meanwhile, in a small bowl combine the alioli ingredients. Mix well.

5. Serve the hot fries with the garlic alioli for dipping.

CHAPTER 4

SOUPS & ONE-POT MEALS

steak *and* bean cowboy chili

ruby reuben bake

creamy kale *and* turkey kielbasa soup

chicken *and* vegetable soup romano

black bean soup

chickpeas *with* chorizo *and* spinach

stuffed peppers *with* sundried tomato sauce

turkey sausage *with* sweet potatoes *and* apricots

baked eggplant puttanesca

chicken potpie

dinner-in-a-salad

paella-style seafood *with* noodles

slow cooker chuck roast *with* root vegetables

polenta verde *with* chicken

salsa verde

chicken *with* artichokes *and* summer vegetables

turkey *and* vegetable puff pie

greek lamb *with* olives *and* feta

steak and bean cowboy chili

Anyone who has ever made chili can testify that if you make a pot of chili, you make a LOT of it. This recipe solves the too-much-chili dilemma, as it makes enough for two generous servings. An electric skillet is perfect for cooking up this spicy dish—we've taken the skillet out on the back deck to prepare this meal alfresco, mixing up the daily routine a bit. Add extra heat by serving with a bottle of your favorite hot sauce.

¾ pound beef chuck boneless steak
2 slices bacon
½ teaspoon dried red pepper flakes*
½ cup chopped onion
½ cup chopped poblano chiles**
½ cup chopped red bell pepper
One 14.5-ounce can diced tomatoes in juice
One 15-ounce can red beans, drained
1 stalk celery, diced
2 cloves garlic, minced
1 teaspoon dried parsley
1 teaspoon ground cumin
½ teaspoon salt
½ teaspoon dried oregano

TOPPINGS (OPTIONAL):
Sour cream
Chopped green onion
Crushed tortilla chips

> **tip**
>
> The meat is easier to cut into cubes when slightly frozen.

1. Cut the meat into ¼-inch cubes. Cut the bacon into ¼-inch pieces.

2. In a large skillet fry the bacon and meat together until both are browned, about 7 minutes. Add the red pepper flakes and onion and sauté until the onions are transparent, about 5 minutes. Add the remaining ingredients (with the exception of the toppings) and simmer on medium heat for 30 minutes, or until half the liquid is absorbed.

3. To serve, ladle the chili into individual bowls and garnish with sour cream, green onions, and tortilla chips.

*   *Reduce or increase the red pepper flakes to the desired heat level.*

**   *Poblano chilies are very mild, but if you prefer, regular green bell pepper can be substituted.*

ruby reuben bake

Now that the kids have flown the coop, you have an opportunity to prepare foods just for the fun of it. Sometimes we just crave something different, and this baked casserole certainly fits the description. The ingredients are nearly identical to a classic Reuben sandwich, but in a baked version. Use leftover home-cooked corned beef in this recipe, but do not use canned corned beef—it's too mushy. Deli corned beef also works well here; just ask your deli to cut it thick for you. A ¼- to ½-inch thick slice is perfect. This is another one of those recipes that will help you use up day-old bread before it goes bad.

> 2 slices rye or wheat bread, cut into 1-inch cubes
> 1½ cups corned beef, diced
> 1½ cups sauerkraut, drained
> 2 tablespoons melted butter
> ¼ cup sour cream
> ¾ cup Swiss cheese, shredded

1. Preheat the oven to 375°F.

2. Place the bread cubes on the bottom of a medium (approximately 4- by 9-inch) baking dish. Sprinkle the corned beef on top of the bread.

3. In a small bowl combine the sauerkraut, butter, and sour cream. Spread this mixture evenly over the bread cubes and beef.

4. Sprinkle the Swiss cheese over the top of the casserole and cover the dish with a piece of aluminum foil. Bake for 20 minutes, or until heated through.

5. Remove the aluminum foil and bake for an additional 5 to 10 minutes, or until the cheese is lightly browned. Serve immediately.

creamy kale and turkey kielbasa soup

If you've never tried kale—a leafy green from the cabbage family—you're in for a treat. Not only is it nutritious (a 3½-ounce serving provides the entire adult daily requirement of vitamins A and C, plus 13 percent of an adult's daily calcium requirement), it's also delicious in soups. In this recipe it's paired with lean turkey sausage, basic pantry vegetables, and red pepper. To lighten it up a bit, use milk instead of cream or half-and-half. We like to prepare this soup during the winter months and park ourselves in front of the fireplace. The bearskin rug is optional.

1 tablespoon olive oil
½ cup chopped onion
½ cup chopped celery
1 cup diced, peeled potatoes (about 1 medium potato)
½ cup chopped, seeded red bell pepper
1 tablespoon all-purpose flour
4 ounces turkey kielbasa sausage (or half a regular kielbasa)*
2 cups chicken stock
2 cups rinsed, chopped kale**
1 cup half-and-half or heavy cream
Salt and freshly ground black pepper

1. Heat the olive oil over medium heat in a large pot. Sauté the onion, celery, potato, and bell pepper until the onions are tender, about 10 minutes. Add the flour and blend thoroughly.

2. While the onions and vegetables are cooking, cut the turkey sausage into ½-inch cubes. Add the sausage to the pot. Add the chicken stock and bring to a boil. Reduce heat to a simmer and add the kale. Simmer for 20 minutes, or until the potatoes and the kale are tender.

3. Add half-and-half and heat through. Do not let the soup come to a boil after adding the cream, as it will begin to separate.

4. Season the soup with salt and pepper to taste and serve hot.

* *Freeze the other half of the sausage and use in the recipe for Turkey Sausage with Sweet Potatoes and Apricots (pages 56–57) on another day.*

** *Kale is very dirty and must be thoroughly cleaned before using. To clean, fill a large bowl with cold water. Submerge the kale in water and swish around to release the dirt. Check the leaves well, as dirt hides in all the curly edges. Remove the kale from the water and pat dry with a clean towel.*

chicken and vegetable soup romano

A *healthy meal-in-a-pot that's great for using up leftover chicken! You can also substitute any fresh seasonal vegetables for the ones used here, and when you're in a pinch or short on time, you can even use a bag of frozen mixed vegetables. The soup cooks quickly and makes a great weeknight supper for busy boomers, especially when accompanied by a loaf of crusty bread for sopping up the last drops. It's also a nice treat for those days when one of you is feeling under the weather.*

1 tablespoon olive oil
½ teaspoon red pepper flakes
½ cup chopped onion
½ cup chopped celery
2 cloves garlic, minced
¼ cup chopped green bell pepper
½ cup sliced carrots
¾ cup diced tomatoes in juice (half a 14.5-ounce can)
2 cups chicken broth (one 14-ounce can)
¾ cup water
¼ cup small shells or elbow macaroni*
1 cup diced, cooked chicken
½ cup fresh cooked or canned garbanzos**
¾ cup sliced zucchini
¾ cup sliced yellow squash
½ cup fresh or frozen green beans
½ teaspoon dried oregano
Salt and freshly ground black pepper

1. Heat the oil in a medium pan with a fitted lid. Add the red pepper flakes and toast them for 1 minute to bring out their flavor. Add the onion, celery, garlic, and green pepper. Cook until onions are transparent, about 10 minutes.

2. Add the carrots, tomatoes, chicken broth, and water. Add the pasta and let the liquid come to a boil over medium-high heat. Turn the heat down to a simmer. Add the chicken, garbanzos, and the remaining vegetables. Simmer for 15 minutes, or until the pasta is soft, adding the oregano during the last 5 minutes of cooking. Season with salt and pepper to taste and serve.

*   *Use small pasta varieties in this soup so it will cook quickly.*

** *One small can or half of a 15-ounce can of garbanzos. In a pinch, you can substitute cooked Great Northern or white beans.*

black bean soup

When I ask my husband what he's craving for dinner on a cold day, his usual reply is "black bean soup," which he likes to prepare himself. But scaling down a bean soup recipe for two is a daunting task, so consider this recipe to be perfect for two hearty appetites. Reheat any leftovers the next day for lunch, or purée them and use as a dip for tortilla chips.

> 2 tablespoons olive oil
> ½ cup chopped onion
> ½ cup chopped celery
> ½ cup seeded and chopped poblano chile or green bell pepper
> ¼ teaspoon red pepper flakes
> 2 cloves garlic, thinly sliced
> 1 medium Roma tomato, seeded and chopped
> 1 teaspoon ground cumin
> 2 cups chicken stock
> 1 cup dried black beans, rinsed and picked through
> ½ cup queso fresco, Cotija, or shredded Monterey Jack cheese*

1. In a medium pot, heat the oil over medium-high heat. Add the onion, celery, and chile and sauté until the onions are transparent, about 5 minutes. Add the red pepper flakes, garlic, and tomato and cook for 1 minute. Add the cumin, chicken stock, and black beans to the pan.

2. Bring the soup to a boil, then reduce heat to medium-low and simmer. Cook uncovered for 1½ to 2 hours**, or until the black beans are tender. If the beans start to look a little dry, add a little water.

3. Remove ½ cup of the bean mixture, place it in a heatproof bowl, and purée using an immersion blender. Return the purée to the soup.

4. Serve in individual serving bowls topped with ¼ cup of the queso fresco.

* *Queso fresco and Cotija are available in stores that carry Hispanic groceries and can be found in the fresh dairy section.*

** *The longer your dried beans are stored in your pantry, the longer they will take to cook, hence the range of cooking time.*

chickpeas with chorizo and spinach

Chickpeas, also called garbanzos and ceci beans, are a common ingredient in Spanish, Italian, and Middle Eastern cooking. Although available dried, they are most often found in cans with other canned beans at the grocery store. It's nice to keep both dried and canned versions in the pantry. The dried chickpeas are soaked and cooked like any other dried bean and, when cooked, can be used interchangeably with the canned version. This recipe is heavy on the garlic—fair warning—but oh, so good!

One 15-ounce can chickpeas
2 tablespoons olive oil
1 cup diced onion
½ cup diced chorizo, andouille, or linguica sausage*
4 cloves garlic, minced
½ teaspoon red pepper flakes
½ cup white wine
2 cups fresh baby spinach
Salt and pepper

1. Rinse the chickpeas under cold running water and drain well. Set aside.

2. In a large skillet heat the oil over medium-high heat. Add the onion and chorizo and cook until the onions are transparent, about 5 minutes. Add the garlic and red pepper flakes, stirring constantly until the garlic just barely begins to brown, about 2 minutes. Add the wine and chickpeas and cook until heated through. Add the spinach and cook about 2–3 minutes until the spinach begins to wilt; don't allow the spinach to become soggy. Season with salt and pepper to taste and serve immediately.

* *Any fully cooked, smoked, paprika-based sausage can be substituted. Do not, however, use fresh Mexican-style chorizo—it's an uncooked sausage that has the consistency of ground meat and is too soft and wet for this recipe.*

stuffed peppers with sun-dried tomato sauce

When my parents were young and us kids were away at our grandparents for a visit, my parents went a little wild, having the house all to themselves for a few days. Dad loved to prepare stuffed bell peppers for my mom during these times—it was their special, romantic meal, and it simply was not made for family occasions. I always thought this was very sweet and tried to have similar traditions when our own kids were away. However, now that it's just us, we can treat every meal as special and romantic! Dad never actually had a written recipe so I had to experiment and improvise to create one that was similar to his. I've used sun-dried tomato paste instead of tomato sauce in this recipe—it gives the filling a more intense tomato flavor.

> 2 tablespoons olive oil, divided
> ½ pound extra-lean ground beef or ground chuck
> ½ cup finely chopped onion
> 2 teaspoons of your favorite bottled chipotle pepper sauce*
> ½ teaspoon salt, plus more to taste
> ¼ teaspoon black pepper
> 3 tablespoons sun-dried tomato paste, divided
> 1 egg, beaten
> 1 cup precooked rice at room temperature**
> 2 bell peppers (any color)
> ¼ cup sour cream
> 1 tablespoon water
> 1 tablespoon lime juice

1. Preheat oven to 425°F.

2. Heat one tablespoon of the olive oil in a medium skillet over high heat. Add the ground beef and cook until browned, about 10 minutes. Add the onion, pepper sauce, salt, pepper, and 2 tablespoons of the sun-dried tomato paste and combine well. Remove the pan from the heat and set aside.

3. Stir the egg into the rice. Add the rice mixture to the meat mixture, combining well.

4. Cut each pepper in half lengthwise and remove the stems and seeds. Place the 4 pepper halves in a small baking dish, with the cavity facing up. Fill each pepper half with the rice/meat mixture. Cover the pan loosely with aluminum foil and bake for 20 minutes. Remove the foil and bake an additional 5 to 7 minutes, or until the filling is lightly browned.

5. While the peppers are roasting, combine the remaining olive oil and sun-dried tomato paste in a small bowl. Add the sour cream, water, and lime juice. Season with salt to taste.

6. Serve the peppers with the sauce.

* *If you don't have chipotle pepper sauce, any red pepper sauce will do, including Tabasco.*
** *This is a terrific recipe for using leftover rice.*

turkey sausage with
sweet potatoes and apricots

Legend has it that Christopher Columbus himself introduced the sweet potato to Europe after discovering it in the New World. The tuber quickly gained popularity, especially among the nobility, and it was considered—you guessed it—an aphrodisiac. So important were these tubers to a successful marriage that they were even included in Catherine of Aragon's dowry when she married England's King Henry VIII. Obviously, they didn't work as intended, because Catherine was only one of Henry's string of wives. Sweet potatoes pair beautifully with sausage, and this recipe is wonderful on a cold day, warming you both from the inside out. It's also quick to prepare. You can wrap and freeze the other half of the sausage and use it in the recipe for Creamy Kale and Turkey Kielbasa Soup (pages 48–49).

1 cup dried apricots
2 cups hot water
4 ounces turkey kielbasa sausage (or half a regular kielbasa)
2 teaspoons vegetable oil
½ cup chopped onion
1 medium sweet potato, peeled and cut into 1-inch cubes*
½ teaspoon salt
¼ teaspoon ground black pepper
2 tablespoons brown sugar
¼ cup water
1 tablespoon bourbon

1. Soak the dried apricots in the hot water for 20 minutes.

2. Cut the sausage into 2-inch sections and brown them in a nonstick skillet over medium-high heat, about 5 to 7 minutes. Add the vegetable oil, onion, and sweet potato. Sauté until the onions and sweet potatoes are lightly browned, about 10 minutes. Drain the apricots and add them to the pan.

3. In a small bowl combine the remaining ingredients. Pour the mixture into the skillet and bring to a boil. Reduce the heat and simmer for about 5 minutes, or until the liquid is slightly reduced, stirring often but being careful not to crush the sweet potatoes.

* *To keep the peeled and cubed sweet potatoes from turning brown until you are ready for them, place them in a bowl of ice water. Drain the water before adding them to the pan.*

baked eggplant puttanesca

We love eggplant in any way, shape, or form. In this recipe it has been combined with another of our favorites—puttanesca sauce. The name alone implies an illicit encounter (puttanesca is the Italian word for a "lady of the evening"), making this a fun dish to prepare for a romantic evening at home. A little role-playing might be in order (and is highly recommended), so break out the stiletto heels or that miniskirt that you've kept in the back of your closet since the seventies and have some fun. Because eggplant tends to soak up oil like a sponge, I have browned and crisped the eggplant in the oven rather than by frying it in a pan. If you're not a fan of eggplant, you can substitute large zucchini or use the sauce recipe in the traditional manner and serve it over hot pasta.

FOR THE SAUCE:

1 tablespoon olive oil

¼ cup chopped onion

½ teaspoon red pepper flakes

2 cloves garlic, minced

One 14-ounce can crushed tomatoes

2 to 3 anchovy fillets, crushed*

1 tablespoon capers

2 tablespoons kalamata olives, pitted and chopped

½ teaspoon salt

1 tablespoon fresh Italian or regular parsley

FOR THE EGGPLANT:

1 large egg

1 tablespoon water

1½ cups seasoned dry bread crumbs

1 medium globe eggplant

Olive oil cooking spray

1. In a medium saucepan heat the olive oil over medium-high heat.

2. Add the onion and red pepper flakes and cook until the onions are transparent, about 5 minutes. Add the garlic and cook until it begins to brown slightly, about 2 minutes. Add the tomatoes and anchovies and cook for 10 minutes, or until the sauce is reduced by almost half. Add the capers, olives, and salt. Reserve the parsley for plating. Keep the sauce warm while preparing the eggplant.

3. Preheat the oven to 400°F. In a medium bowl beat the egg with the water. Place the bread crumbs in a second medium bowl. Cut the eggplant into ¾-inch-thick slices. Dip each slice in the egg mixture and then into the bread crumbs, coating thoroughly.

4. Place the slices on a baking sheet and spray with the cooking spray. Turn the slices over and spray the other sides. Bake the eggplant slices for 7 to 10 minutes, turning once, or until golden brown and crispy.

5. Arrange the eggplant slices on a serving platter. Top with the sauce and sprinkle with the reserved parsley.

*   *You can substitute 2 teaspoons of anchovy paste.*

chicken potpie

When my husband and I began dating way back when, he subsisted mainly on beer and frozen pot-pies. I recall one "memorable" date night when we strolled along Huntington Beach, walked back to his place, and had dinner, which he made himself. From a tin foil pan, I was served an oozing mess of a chicken potpie that tasted like a cross between a piece of cardboard and my pillow. Not exactly gourmet, but romantic nonetheless. Luckily we developed our own recipes and never had to eat cardboard potpies again. This version of potpie can best be described as halfway between a potpie and chicken with dumplings. You can easily substitute other vegetables for the ones in this recipe; it can be a wonderful way to clean out small quantities of veggies lurking in the fridge. This recipe can serve two hearty appetites or provide leftovers for lunch.

FOR THE FILLING:

2 boneless, skinless chicken breasts
1 tablespoon olive oil
1 cup coarsely chopped onion
1 cup thinly sliced carrots
1 cup thinly sliced celery
¼ cup diced red bell pepper
¾ cup green beans, cut into 1-inch lengths
½ teaspoon salt
¼ teaspoon freshly ground black pepper
1 tablespoon all-purpose flour
1½ cups chicken stock
½ cup milk
½ teaspoon dried thyme
¼ teaspoon dried rosemary, crushed

FOR THE TOPPING:

¾ cup all-purpose flour
1 teaspoon baking powder
¼ teaspoon salt
1 egg, beaten
1 tablespoon olive oil
¼ cup milk

1. Preheat the oven to 425°F.

2. Cut the two chicken breasts into 1-inch cubes. Heat the olive oil in a medium skillet over medium-high heat and brown the chicken cubes on all sides, about 20 minutes.

3. In a lidded medium baking dish combine the vegetables. Remove the chicken from the skillet, reserving the oil, and place the chicken in the baking dish with the vegetables. Add the salt and pepper.

4. Return the pan with remaining oil to the stove. Stir the flour into the oil and add the chicken stock and milk, stirring constantly until the mixture begins to thicken, about 5 to 7 minutes. Add the thyme and rosemary. Pour the hot liquid mixture over the chicken and vegetables.

5. Combine the ingredients for the topping in a medium bowl. Cover the meat and vegetable mixture with the topping. Place the lid on the dish and bake covered for 20 minutes, or until the topping begins to set in the middle. Remove the lid and bake an additional 5 to 7 minutes, until the topping begins to brown.

dinner-in-a-salad

If you've ever enjoyed a BLT&E (bacon, lettuce, and tomato sandwich with an egg) for dinner, you're going to love this salad. It combines all the classic BLT&E components with a delicious herbed mayonnaise dressing. Super-simple and ready in a flash, it's perfect for a lazy at-home night or even for a romantic brunch or breakfast in bed.

FOR THE SALAD:

¼ pound of thick-cut bacon (about 5 or 6 strips)
½ romaine lettuce head, rinsed and dried
½ pint container of cherry or grape tomatoes
¼ cup thinly sliced red onion
4 slices French or Italian bread, ½ inch thick, toasted and buttered
2 large eggs
Salt and pepper

FOR THE DRESSING:

⅓ cup mayonnaise
1 tablespoon white vinegar
1 teaspoon dried basil, crushed
¼ teaspoon dried parsley
1 clove garlic, minced

1. In a large skillet cook the bacon over medium heat until crispy. While the bacon is frying, tear the lettuce into bite-size pieces and divide between two serving plates. Top each plate with half of the tomatoes and red onion slices.

2. Place two slices of the toasted bread on the side of each serving plate, overlapping the salad. Remove the bacon from the skillet with a slotted spoon, drain on paper towels, then crumble. Fry the two eggs in the pan drippings: cook them sunny-side up (without turning) or over easy (turned).

3. While the eggs are cooking, in a small bowl combine the dressing ingredients. Season the eggs with salt and pepper to taste. Place one egg and half of the crumbled bacon on each salad and pour the dressing over the top. Serve immediately.

paella-style seafood with noodles

My husband is a big fan of well-made paella, but it can be difficult to scale such a grand meal for just two eaters. We both especially enjoyed the paella my grandfather would make. My abuelo, a short, bald, blue-eyed butterball from the Canary Islands, was a whiz in the kitchen, and I learned so much from him—especially that food was a pleasure and a joy, and that quality ingredients make the difference between an everyday dish and something truly special.

I loved to sit on a stool and watch the master at work. From my perch, I learned techniques passed down through the generations that are more valuable than any cooking school techniques I have learned. Who but my grandfather knew that you could seal an oven door shut with aluminum foil when the round, flat-bottomed pan used for cooking the paella was too big to fit in the oven? Of course, he would rather have cooked the paella outside over an open fire, but with Washington being the rain capital of the West, the oven had to do.

In this recipe, I have taken the spirit of making paella and translated it into a meal for two using excellent ingredients (spoil yourself), sun-ripened tomatoes, and fresh pasta.

1 tablespoon plus 1 teaspoon salt
One 9-ounce package fresh linguine (from the deli case)
1 generous pinch of saffron threads, crushed
2 tablespoons olive oil
½ cup fresh ripe tomatoes, seeded and diced
1 cup chopped onion
½ cup chopped red bell pepper*
2 cloves garlic, finely minced
½ cup dry white wine or sherry
½ pound shrimp, peeled and deveined
1 pound clams in their shells, cleaned
½ cup fresh or frozen peas

1. In a large pan, bring 4 quarts of water to a boil and add the tablespoon of salt. Cook the pasta until tender according to the package directions. Drain the pasta and keep it warm.

2. While the pasta is cooking, start the sauce. Heat a large skillet over medium heat. Add the saffron threads and toast them lightly, being careful not to let them burn. Add the oil, tomatoes, onion, and bell pepper. Cook this mixture until the onions become soft, about 5 to 7 minutes. Add the remaining salt, the garlic, and the wine, reduce heat to medium-low, and bring to a simmer.

3. Add the shrimp and clams to the pan and cover lightly to allow them to steam. When the clams have opened, after about 8 to 10 minutes, and the shrimp are pink, add the peas.

4. Place the pasta in a serving platter and top with the seafood mixture. Before serving, remove any clams that have failed to open.

* *Jarred or canned pimientos or red peppers can be substituted for the fresh bell pepper.*

slow cooker chuck roast
with root vegetables

Plug in the slow cooker and escape with your mate for a playdate! Using a slow cooker is a great way to have a wonderful home-cooked meal on a busy day when you're indulging each other in your favorite pastimes. Assemble the ingredients the night before or in the morning, plug the cooker in, and forget it. When you walk in the door after a hard day of goofing around, you'll be greeted by the wonderful sauerbraten-like aroma and the knowledge that dinner's ready without any hassle. Since it's difficult to get a roast sized for two, you may have a bit left over—or not, depending on your appetite. This is delicious served with white rice.

One 2-pound chuck roast
Salt and pepper
1 small onion, cut into ¼-inch-thick slices
2 ribs of celery, cut into 2-inch lengths
2 carrots, cut into 1-inch chunks
2 turnips, cut into 1-inch chunks
One 8-ounce can tomato sauce
¼ cup brown sugar
2 tablespoons red wine vinegar
1 teaspoon prepared mustard
Dash of ground cinnamon

1. Season the meat with salt and pepper on all sides. Place the onion, celery, carrots, and turnips at the bottom of the slow cooker. Place the meat on top of the vegetables.

2. Combine the remaining ingredients in a small bowl. Pour the tomato sauce mixture over the meat. Cook on the medium setting for 9 to 10 hours, or until the meat is tender.

polenta verde with chicken

his recipe was born out of necessity on a day that we were both craving chicken enchiladas verdes but had run out of tortillas. After digging through the newly organized pantry, I remembered that we had a nice bag of organic polenta tucked in the back—perfect! Since we were both short on time, we chose to microwave the polenta. You can use leftover chicken, and in no time you'll have a quick, satisfying meal. I have supplied a recipe for Salsa Verde (page 70), but you can also use green salsa from a can or jar if you have it available.

½ cup polenta (not cornmeal)
2½ cups water
½ teaspoon salt
1 cup shredded cooked chicken
½ cup diced onion
¾ cup shredded Monterey Jack cheese
¼ cup sour cream
2 tablespoons sliced black olives
½ cup mild or medium salsa verde

1. Put the polenta, water, and salt in a large heatproof bowl. Microwave on high heat for 3 minutes. Stir the polenta with a whisk and microwave on high for an additional 3 minutes. The polenta at this stage will be creamy and ready to spoon onto plates. As the polenta cools, it will set up. Divide the polenta between two plates.

2. Top the polenta on each plate with half of each of the remaining ingredients and serve.

salsa verde

Making your own green salsa is easy and is a great way to get your significant other cooking along with you. While you're stirring the polenta, have him or her prepare this tasty accompaniment.

2 seeded, diced jalapeños*
One 12-ounce can whole tomatillos, drained
1 teaspoon minced garlic
½ cup chopped onion
½ cup white vinegar
1 teaspoon salt

Place all the ingredients in a blender and purée. Serve with Polenta Verde with Chicken (page 69) or use as a dip for chips. Refrigerate unused portion for up to 4 days.

* *You can reserve some or all of the seeds to kick up the "heat."*

chicken with artichokes and summer vegetables

Baby vegetables are popping up in more grocery stores these days. They're a bit more expensive than their full-sized counterparts, but they're worth it from both a flavor and presentation standpoint. The miniature versions just look downright adorable and extravagant on our plates. We can't help but feel special eating them. If you are unable to find baby vegetables, full-sized versions can be cut into small pieces and used instead.

    1 tablespoon olive oil
    ¾ pound chicken tenders
    ½ cup chopped onion
    1 clove garlic, minced
    One 14-ounce can artichoke hearts*
    ¾ to 1 pound of assorted baby vegetables, which can include pattypan squash,
        green zucchini, sugar snap peas, beets, cauliflower, and baby carrots
    ½ cup yellow beans, cut in 1-inch lengths
    2 tablespoons Dijon-style mustard
    1 teaspoon Worcestershire sauce
    ¼ cup dry white wine

In a large skillet, heat the oil over medium-high heat. Brown the chicken on all sides, about 15 minutes. Add the onion, garlic, artichokes, baby vegetables, and beans. Sauté for 5 to 7 minutes, or until the vegetables are cooked, but not mushy. Combine the remaining ingredients and pour over the meat and vegetables in the pan. Heat until bubbly and serve.

*   *Don't use pickled artichoke hearts here—the pickled flavor will overpower the fresh vegetables.*

turkey and vegetable puff pie

Most empty nesters—ourselves included—often find themselves with a lot of leftovers. This soufflé-like dish is a great way to use up some of those leftovers and works equally well with chicken. Raid the fridge for leftover vegetables as well. To give it a little extra kick, use pepper Jack cheese in place of the Monterey Jack.

Nonstick cooking spray
2 large eggs
½ cup milk
½ cup all-purpose flour
¼ teaspoon salt
Dash of freshly ground black pepper
½ teaspoon Worcestershire sauce
1 clove garlic, crushed
½ cup grated Monterey Jack or pepper Jack cheese
1 cup shredded cooked turkey
One 10-ounce package frozen chopped spinach
¼ cup chopped onion
¼ cup finely diced carrots
½ cup corn
¼ cup diced green bell pepper

1. Preheat the oven to 425°F and coat the inside of a 2-quart casserole dish with the cooking spray.

2. In a medium bowl beat the eggs and add the milk, flour, salt, pepper, Worcestershire sauce, and garlic. Beat in the Monterey Jack.

3. Combine the remaining ingredients in the casserole dish. Pour the egg mixture over the turkey and vegetables. Bake for 20 to 25 minutes, or until the top of the casserole is lightly browned and puffy.

greek lamb with olives and feta

Spring lamb is perfect for this rustic dish. The aroma will instantly transport you to the Greek isles, where you can picture you and your love wearing nothing more than beach sand. If you can't be there in body, you may as well be there in spirit. Serve this dish with crusty country-style bread and a nice Shiraz (Syrah) or cabernet.

½ pound lamb, cut into 1-inch cubes
Salt and pepper
2 tablespoons flour
1 tablespoon olive oil
1 large onion, quartered
1 large potato, peeled and cut into 1-inch cubes
1 medium lemon
2 cloves garlic, crushed
One 8-ounce can tomato sauce
1 teaspoon dried oregano
¼ teaspoon dried rosemary, crushed
½ cup kalamata olives, pitted and halved
½ cup crumbled feta cheese

1. Season the lamb cubes with salt and pepper to taste. In a small bowl, toss the lamb with the flour to coat.

2. In a 3- or 4-quart Dutch oven, heat the olive oil over medium-high heat. Add the lamb and brown on all sides, about 10 minutes. Add the onion and potato and cook until the potatoes are lightly browned, about 15 minutes.

3. Remove 1 teaspoon of zest from the lemon and reserve. Squeeze the juice, adding water if necessary to make ¼ cup of liquid. Add the lemon juice, garlic, tomato sauce, oregano, rosemary, and olives to the pot. Bring to a boil, reduce the heat to low, and cover. Continue to cook over low heat on top of the stove for 30 minutes, stirring occasionally but being careful not to break the potatoes, until the lamb is tender.

4. To serve, spoon the lamb and vegetable mixture into two serving bowls. Toss the crumbled feta with the reserved lemon zest and sprinkle half of the feta mixture over each serving.

CHAPTER 5

MEAT & POULTRY

turkey schnitzel *with* mustard sauce

cuban-style pork steaks *with* avocado jicama salsa

sunday chicken

grilled citrus chicken satay

grilled skirt steak

beef tips *in* red wine tarragon sauce

grilled garlic *and* lemon lamb chops

pan-fried pork chops *in* cumin tomato sauce

chicken tenders piccata style

pan-fried pork medallions *with* eve's apples

chicken *and* rice meatballs marsala

mini italian-style meat loaves

bourbon-roasted rock cornish hens

grilled buffalo 'shroom burgers

grilled pork *and* pineapple lettuce wraps

turkey croquettes *with* creole dipping sauce

new york strip steak salad *with* spinach *and* strawberries

herb-crusted rack of lamb

tenderloin steaks au poivre

pork sirloin tips montreal

turkey schnitzel with mustard sauce

Schnitzel is a common dish in Germany and refers to any meat that has been pounded thin. While you may be most familiar with veal schnitzel, pork, beef, chicken—and, in this case, turkey—can also be used. The mustard sauce gives it a ton of flavor and can double as a zippy salad dressing. This is one of my favorite meals to prepare with my husband. He likes to do the pounding while I dredge, and he prepares the sauce as I cook.

½ package (about ¾ pound) turkey breast cutlets
Salt and pepper
1 large egg
1 tablespoon water
1½ cups Italian-style or plain dry bread crumbs
½ cup canola oil
⅓ cup heavy cream
¼ cup prepared Dijon mustard
1 teaspoon capers (optional)

> ### tip
> Schnitzel should be eaten as soon as it is removed from the pan, as it tends to "wilt" if left sitting on a serving platter for too long.

1. Sandwich the cutlets between sheets of waxed paper and pound them with a meat mallet or rolling pin until they are about ¼ inch thick. Season them to taste with salt and pepper.

2. In a wide, shallow pan or bowl, combine the egg and water. Beat well to combine. Place the bread crumbs in a second shallow pan. Heat the oil in a large nonstick skillet.

3. Dip cutlets in the egg mixture, coating both sides. Then dip them in the bread crumbs, making sure they are completely coated. Fry each cutlet until golden brown, about 3 minutes on each side. Do not crowd the pan. You may only be able to fit one cutlet in the pan at a time; keep the cooked cutlets warm in a 300-degree oven. After frying, remove the cutlets from the skillet with a slotted spatula and drain on paper towels.

4. To make the sauce, combine the heavy cream, Dijon mustard, and capers. Serve the sauce on the side or pour it over the cutlets.

cuban-style pork steaks with avocado jicama salsa

This recipe is wonderful with pork shoulder steaks, but pork loin or rib chops work equally well. You can make the salsa and put the pork in the marinade earlier in the day and keep them both in the refrigerator to let the flavors meld. Take advantage of your free time together by planning an excursion, and let the meat and salsa take care of themselves while you're gone—just grill the meat when you get home and serve.

FOR THE STEAKS:

1 tablespoon olive oil

2 tablespoons lemon juice

½ teaspoon cayenne

1 teaspoon ground cumin

¼ teaspoon salt

¼ teaspoon freshly ground black pepper

1 teaspoon onion powder

2 cloves garlic, minced

2 bone-in pork blade steaks or loin chops, ¼ to ½ inches thick

FOR THE SALSA:

1 ripe avocado, peeled, pitted, and diced

1 small jicama, peeled and diced into ¼-inch cubes

1 small tomato, seeded and finely chopped

¼ cup finely chopped onion

Juice of one medium lime (about 2 tablespoons)

1 tablespoon chopped fresh cilantro

Dash of cayenne

1. Combine all steak ingredients except the pork in a large zipper-top plastic bag. Seal the pork steaks in the bag and allow them to marinate for at least one hour.

2. Meanwhile, make the salsa by combining all of the ingredients in a medium bowl. Chill until the steaks are ready.

3. Preheat indoor or outdoor grill to high heat. Remove steaks from bag and grill on high heat for 3 minutes on each side, or until cooked through.

4. Remove from grill and allow the meat to rest for 5 minutes. Serve the steaks with the salsa.

sunday chicken

This recipe takes its name from the traditional chicken my grandmother would cook on Sundays. Redolent of garlic and herbs, it's still one of my favorite comfort foods. Reduce or increase the number of garlic cloves based on your own personal taste preferences. We like ours loaded with garlic, especially since we read somewhere that garlic is considered a "hot" herb that fuels desire. Whether it does or does not fuel passion, it definitely helps if you eat it together, given the breath factor. Kiss, kiss!

1 tablespoon olive oil
Juice of one medium lemon (about ¼ cup)
½ teaspoon dried oregano
½ teaspoon rubbed sage
6 cloves garlic, thinly sliced
½ cup chopped onion
1 teaspoon paprika
Salt and pepper
2 chicken breast halves

1. In a small bowl combine all the ingredients except the salt, pepper, and chicken. Season the oil mixture with salt and pepper to taste.

2. Place the chicken breasts in a shallow baking dish. Rub the oil mixture onto all sides of the chicken breasts and then pour any remaining oil mixture over the chicken. Bake for 20 to 25 minutes, or until the chicken is cooked through and the skin is crispy.

grilled citrus chicken satay

Togetherness is bliss. You can easily divide the cooking chores in this recipe by having one person slice and skewer the meat while the other prepares the luscious citrus-based ponzu sauce. A perfect accompaniment to this dish is the Asian Summer Salad (page 26), and it makes for a light, refreshing summer meal.

2 small boneless, skinless chicken breasts (or one large breast)

FOR THE SAUCE:

Juice of one medium orange (about ⅓ cup)
1 tablespoon orange zest
½ cup soy sauce
2 tablespoons rice wine vinegar
½ teaspoon sesame oil
1 clove garlic, minced
1 tablespoon brown sugar

1. Preheat indoor or outdoor grill to high heat.

2. Soak six 8-inch bamboo skewers in water for 10 minutes—this will keep them from burning when placed on the grill. Slice the chicken into three strips along the length of the breast. Thread each strip of chicken onto a skewer. Place the skewers in a shallow dish.

3. For the ponzu sauce, combine the remaining ingredients in a medium bowl. Pour half of the sauce over the chicken skewers and let them stand for 20 minutes in the refrigerator to marinate, turning the skewers often. Reserve the other half of the sauce for serving.

4. Place the chicken skewers on the grill, discarding the sauce used as a marinade. Grill the skewers for 2 to 3 minutes on each side, or until thoroughly cooked. Serve with the reserved sauce.

grilled skirt steak

Skirt steak is a little harder to find than other cuts of beef, but it is well worth the effort. It comes from the diaphragm muscle, and at first glance may look tough, but it's extremely tender and flavorful—one of my favorite cuts for grilling. If you can't find it in the meat case, ask your butcher. Serve with warm flour or corn tortillas, refried beans, salsa, Tijuana Rice (page 173), or with any of your other favorite sides. We like to use the leftover meat in a salad, eliminating cooking for an evening and giving the two of us more time together for activities involving bubbles and bathwater.

¾ pound skirt steak
Juice of one medium lime (about 2 tablespoons)
2 tablespoons Dijon-style mustard
1 tablespoon olive oil
2 tablespoons white vinegar
1 glove garlic, mashed into a paste
¼ teaspoon ground coriander
½ teaspoon granulated onion
½ teaspoon salt
¼ teaspoon black pepper

1. Trim away the surface fat and silver skin (the thin, white membrane) from the meat. Place the remaining ingredients in a large zipper-top bag and combine well. Place the bag in the refrigerator to marinate for 2 to 6 hours.

2. Preheat indoor or outdoor grill to high heat. Remove the meat from the bag and grill for 1 to 2 minutes on each side for medium.

3. Place the meat on a platter and let it rest for 5 minutes. Slice across the grain to serve.

beef tips in red wine tarragon sauce

Pull out your best china and crystal, because these tender, juicy beef tenderloin tips are perfect for a fancy Sunday dinner for two. Traditionally this dish is served on a bed of hot rice or your favorite noodles, but you may also use a rustic, crusty bread to soak up the delicious sauce. A small green salad rounds out the meal, and a deep red wine, such as a pinot noir or a cabernet, goes nicely with this dish.

1 tablespoon olive oil
½ pound beef tips, cut into 1-inch cubes
Salt and pepper
1 tablespoon all-purpose flour
½ teaspoon unsalted butter
½ cup chopped onion
1 clove garlic, sliced
½ cup dry red wine
½ cup beef broth
1 teaspoon fresh chopped tarragon

tip

The sauce will thicken in the pan as the meat cooks. If the mixture becomes too thick, you can thin it with a little bit of extra beef stock or wine. If the sauce is not thick enough, remove the lid and reduce the juices a bit more before adding the tarragon.

1. In a 3- to 4-quart Dutch oven, heat the oil over medium-high heat. In a medium bowl season the beef with salt and pepper to taste and toss it with the flour to coat. Add the meat to the pot and brown on all sides, about 10 minutes. Remove the meat from the pot and set aside.

2. In the same pot, add the butter, onion, and garlic and sauté until the onions are transparent, about 5 minutes. Put the meat back in the pot and add the wine and beef broth. Bring to a boil, then reduce heat to medium-low. Cover loosely and simmer for 20 minutes, or until the meat is tender.

3. Add the tarragon and simmer for an additional 5 minutes. Serve over hot rice or wide noodles.

grilled garlic and lemon lamb chops

Lamb, lemon, and garlic are common ingredients in Middle Eastern cooking. The dried thyme gives this dish a heady herbal aroma while the lemon adds zing. Casanova—the infamous "Great Lover"—thought of lemons as a "miraculous aphrodisiac," which makes this a fitting meal for a night filled with romance. Cooking this dish can be fun as well—my husband loves to man the grill while I prepare Couscous with Sautéed Vegetables (page 165) as an accompaniment.

4 lamb loin chops, 1-inch thick*
1 tablespoon olive oil
2 teaspoons fresh lemon juice
¼ teaspoon salt
Dash of pepper
1 teaspoon dried thyme
1 clove garlic, minced

1. Place the lamb chops in a plastic zipper-top bag. Add the remaining ingredients, seal the top, and shake the bag to combine well. Refrigerate for 1 hour to allow the marinade to permeate the meat.

2. Preheat indoor or outdoor grill to high heat. Grill the chops for 5 minutes on each side for medium doneness.

* *Lamb loin chops look like miniature T-bone steaks. Rib or sirloin chops, medallions, or noisettes can be used in place of the loin chops.*

pan-fried pork chops
in cumin tomato sauce

Hearty and satisfying, this cumin-infused dish pairs beautifully with potatoes or rice. It's perfect for a winter evening in front of a roaring fire. I think of cumin as a sexy spice because of its heady, musky aroma. In the Middle Ages, cumin symbolized love and fidelity and was often carried in the pockets of people attending weddings, as a means of wishing the couple a happy life together. A bottle of pinot gris pairs well with this dish.

1 tablespoon olive oil
2 top loin chops, about 1 inch thick
½ cup chopped onion
½ cup thinly sliced celery
1 clove garlic, crushed
½ teaspoon ground cumin
½ teaspoon salt
¼ teaspoon black pepper
One 14.5-ounce can crushed tomatoes
Juice of one medium lime (about 2 tablespoons)

tip
Ask your butcher for two nice, thick top loin chops (also called center cut) for this recipe. They'll cook up meaty and tender. Rib chops or blade chops often cook up too dry or tough.

1. Heat the oil in a large skillet over medium heat. Add the pork chops and brown them on both sides, about 5 minutes per side. Remove the pork from the pan and keep it warm while preparing the sauce.

2. Add the onion and celery to the pan and sauté until the onions are transparent, about 5 minutes. Add the garlic, cumin, salt, and pepper and cook for 1 minute. Return the pork chops to the pan and turn to coat. Pour the tomatoes and lime juice over the pork chops. Simmer for 15 to 20 minutes, turning the pork chops occasionally until thoroughly cooked through.

MEAT & POULTRY

chicken tenders piccata style

*C*hicken tenders are perfect for this recipe. They are naturally tender without having to be pounded and will cut your preparation time in half, making this dish perfect for busy weeknights when you would rather spend time together than cook a time-consuming meal. You can still use regular boneless, skinless breasts if you wish, pounding them thinly between sheets of waxed paper. Boneless pork chops and turkey or veal cutlets also work well with this recipe.

¾ pound fresh chicken tenders
Salt and pepper
1 tablespoon olive oil
¼ cup chicken broth*
2 tablespoons dry white wine
1 tablespoon freshly squeezed lemon juice
¼ teaspoon lemon zest
1 tablespoon capers**
2 tablespoons chopped fresh or dried parsley

1. Sprinkle the chicken tenders with salt and pepper to taste.

2. Heat the oil in a large skillet over medium-high heat and add the chicken tenders. Cook the tenders until browned and thoroughly cooked, about 10 minutes. Remove the chicken from the pan and keep warm on a serving platter.

3. Reduce the heat to medium. Add the broth and wine to the pan, scraping the browned bits from the bottom. Add the lemon juice, lemon zest, and capers. Simmer the sauce for 1 minute. Spoon the sauce over the chicken and sprinkle with the parsley. Serve immediately.

* *Use ¼ cup hot water and ½ teaspoon of chicken-flavored bouillon if you don't have chicken stock in the fridge.*

** *Use drained pickled capers or rinsed salt-cured capers.*

pan-fried pork medallions
with eve's apples

As its name implies, this is a sweet, seductive dish. The cooking tasks can be easily divided, giving you the perfect opportunity to create this meal as a couple. While one person is preparing the pork, the other can be peeling and slicing the apples—and pouring the champagne.

2 tablespoons butter
Half of a 1½-pound pork loin*
Salt and pepper
2 Granny Smith apples, peeled and cored
2 tablespoons brown sugar
½ teaspoon ground cinnamon
Dash of ground cloves

1. In a large skillet melt the butter over medium-high heat. Cut the pork loin into 1-inch-thick medallions, and season to taste with salt and pepper. Slice the apples into ½-inch-thick slices.

2. Add the pork medallions to the pan and brown on both sides, about 10 minutes per side. Reduce the heat to medium-low and add the brown sugar, stirring to dissolve. Add the apples, cinnamon, and cloves, gently tossing and turning the ingredients in the pan to evenly coat. Cook for 10 minutes, turning frequently, or until the apples are tender but not mushy.

* *This is the standard size of most pork loins available at grocery stores, but it is too large for two people. Cut the pork loin in two, using half for this recipe and the other half for the Grilled Pork and Pineapple Lettuce Wraps (pages 94–95) on another day.*

chicken and rice meatballs marsala

Traditionally, chicken Marsala is heavy on the butter and cream and served with pasta. In this skinnied-down version, lean ground chicken is combined with rice and baked to create low-fat meatballs that are tender and juicy on the inside. A simple sauce with mushrooms, a touch of butter, and Marsala finishes the dish without adding excess fat. This recipe is also a great way to use up a cup of leftover cooked rice.

10 ounces (half a 1.25-pound package) ground chicken*
¼ cup finely chopped onion
½ teaspoon salt
½ teaspoon pepper
1 egg, beaten, at room temperature
1 cup cooked rice
2 tablespoons butter, divided
¼ pound mushrooms, sliced
1 tablespoon flour
½ cup chicken stock
¼ cup dry Marsala**

1. Preheat the oven to 400°F.

2. Combine the chicken, onion, salt, pepper, and egg and mix well. Add the rice and mix until thoroughly combined. Shape into 2-inch balls. Place a baking rack on a large sheet pan. Lightly coat the rack with cooking spray to prevent sticking. Arrange balls on a baking rack, spacing them at least one inch apart. Bake for 30 to 35 minutes, or until cooked through.

3. In a medium skillet, melt one tablespoon of the butter and add the mushroom slices. Sauté until the mushrooms are reduced in size by half, about 7 minutes. Remove the mushrooms from the pan and set aside. Add the remaining butter and melt over medium heat. Add the flour and stir to make a smooth paste. Add the chicken stock and Marsala. Stir until smooth and slightly thickened. Return mushrooms to the pan.

4. Arrange the meatballs on a plate or serving platter and spoon the sauce over the meatballs to serve.

* *Sometimes ground chicken is firmer or moister than at other times. If, after mixing your meatball ingredients together, you feel your mixture is not firm enough to form into balls that will hold their shape, add 1 to 2 tablespoons plain bread crumbs.*

** *You may also use Marsala cooking wine, usually found near the vinegar and cooking sherry.*

mini italian-style meat loaves

*T*ender and moist, these meat loaves will soon become a favorite! For a carefree weeknight meal for two, mix up the ingredients in the morning. When you get home, shape the mixture into loaves and bake. While the meat loaves are cooking, prepare the simple tomato sauce and exchange some of those "I know what you're thinking about" glances with your partner.*

FOR THE MEAT LOAVES:
- ½ pound lean ground beef
- ½ pound ground turkey
- 1 egg, beaten
- ½ cup fine dry bread crumbs
- ½ cup grated Parmesan cheese
- ½ cup finely diced onion
- ¼ cup finely diced green bell pepper
- ½ cup finely diced celery
- ½ teaspoon salt
- ½ teaspoon ground black pepper

FOR THE SAUCE:
- One 8-ounce can tomato sauce
- ½ teaspoon herbes de Provence
- ½ cup grated mozzarella cheese

> ## tip
> These loaves can also be baked in individual casserole dishes or mini loaf pans.

1. Preheat the oven to 350°F.

2. In a medium bowl combine the meat loaf ingredients, mixing well. Divide the mixture into 2 parts and shape each into a loaf shape approximately 3 by 5 inches. Place the two loaves in a shallow baking dish and cover with aluminum foil. Bake for 25 minutes. Remove the foil and bake for an additional 10 minutes, or until golden brown.

3. For the sauce, combine the tomato sauce and the herbes de Provence in a small bowl. Pour the sauce over the meat loaves and sprinkle with the grated mozzarella. Bake just until the cheese has melted and serve.

MEAT & POULTRY

91

bourbon-roasted rock cornish hens

Rock Cornish hens, in my opinion, are an underutilized item in poultrydom. They are quick to cook and can be prepared in the same ways as their larger poultry cousins. The hens are a cross between White Rock hens and Cornish hens. The average weight of a Rock Cornish hen is between 1 and 1½ pounds, making one hen the perfect size for each person. I like to go all out when presenting this dish, placing the two birds on a nest of vegetables or herbs surrounded by tealight candles. There's just something deliciously romantic about two birds for two people.

> 2 frozen Rock Cornish hens, thawed
> 1 orange, quartered
> ¼ cup (½ stick) melted butter
> ¼ cup bourbon*
> 2 tablespoons brown sugar
> 1 teaspoon garlic powder
> ½ teaspoon salt
> ¼ teaspoon freshly ground black pepper
> 4 to 5 small red new potatoes, quartered

1. Preheat the oven to 375°F.

2. Rinse the hens under cold water and pat them dry. Place them in a shallow baking dish. Insert one of the orange quarters into each bird. Tie the legs of each bird closed with kitchen twine and tuck the wing tips to the back of the birds.

3. Combine all remaining ingredients except for the potatoes. Squeeze the juice from the remaining 2 orange quarters into the mixture.

4. Place the hens on a rack in a small roasting pan. Arrange the potatoes around the hens. Brush the hens and potatoes with the bourbon mixture and place the pan in the oven, uncovered.

5. Roast for 45 minutes, basting with additional bourbon mixture every 5 to 10 minutes, until the skin is browned and the hens are cooked through.

* *You may substitute whisky or brandy for the bourbon for a change of pace.*

grilled buffalo 'shroom burgers

These aren't kiddie burgers! No longer having the kids in the house means you can experiment with new takes on your old favorites. Using ground buffalo is definitely a grown-up take on a classic. Ground buffalo makes its appearance in the grocery stores several times a year. It's very lean and low in cholesterol. Because of its low fat content it can cook a little dry, but with the addition of dried and hydrated shiitake mushrooms and grated Parmesan cheese, these burgers turn out juicy and succulent every time. Buffalo is almost 100 percent pure protein, which means it also has very little shrinkage, making it perfect for king-size burgers that will fit jumbo buns.

> 1 pound lean (15 percent fat) ground buffalo
> ½ cup dried shiitake mushrooms, hydrated*
> ¼ cup chopped red onion
> ¼ cup grated Parmesan cheese**
> Salt and pepper

1. Place the ground buffalo in a medium bowl. Coarsely chop the mushrooms and add them to the ground meat along with the onion and Parmesan. Mix well to combine. Season with salt and pepper to taste. Divide the meat mixture in half and form each half into a large patty about ½ inch thick.

2. Preheat indoor or outdoor grill to medium-high heat. Place the patties on the grill and cook for 4 minutes on each side for medium well. Serve them on jumbo buns with your favorite condiments, thinly sliced red onion, lettuce, and tomato.

*   To hydrate the mushrooms, place them in a small bowl with 1½ cups of room temperature water and let them soak for about 10 to 15 minutes, or until soft.

**   The stuff out of the familiar green shaker works best!

grilled pork and pineapple lettuce wraps

If you've never had grilled fresh pineapple, you're in for a treat! It's delicious, and paired with grilled pork loin and a refreshing salsa, this is grilling heaven! Serving the pork, pineapple, and salsa in lettuce leaves makes for a pretty presentation, and the wraps are convenient to eat with one hand, whether you're on the back deck, on the boat, or cuddled up on the sofa. I recommend having a cold glass of rum punch in the opposite hand.

FOR THE PORK:

    Half of a 1½-pound pork loin*

    ½ cup cider vinegar

    Juice of one large orange (about ½ cup)

    1 teaspoon orange zest

    ½ cup packed brown sugar

    1 teaspoon freshly grated ginger

    ½ teaspoon salt

FOR THE PINEAPPLE:

    ½ fresh pineapple, peeled

    ½ teaspoon butter, melted

    1 teaspoon brown sugar

FOR THE SALSA AND WRAPS:

    ¼ cup chopped red onion

    1 cup seeded and chopped Roma tomatoes

    2 tablespoons cider vinegar

    2 tablespoons orange juice

    1 tablespoon brown sugar

    ¼ teaspoon salt

    ½ teaspoon freshly grated ginger

    6 iceberg lettuce leaves

1. In a zipper-top bag combine the pork with the marinade ingredients. Close the top of the bag and massage the contents to combine. Place the bag in the refrigerator and allow the contents to marinate for 2 to 3 hours.

2. Preheat indoor or outdoor grill to high heat. Remove the pork from the bag and discard excess marinade. Place the meat over medium coals and grill for 8 minutes per side, or until internal temperature reaches 145°F. Cut the pork into ½-inch chunks.

3. While the meat is cooking, cut the pineapple into 6 wedges or equal pieces. Rub these pieces with the melted butter and sprinkle with the brown sugar. Place the pineapple on the grill and grill for 3 to 5 minutes, or until lightly browned. Turn often so the pineapple doesn't char. Cut the grilled pineapple into 1-inch chunks.

4. Combine the ingredients for the salsa. Serve by placing a mound of pork on a lettuce leaf and topping it with the pineapple and salsa.

* *Use the second half of the pork loin for Pan-Fried Pork Medallions with Eve's Apples (page 87).*

turkey croquettes with creole dipping sauce

Using leftover turkey or chicken in croquettes is a terrific way to use up meat without it seeming like you're having plain old leftovers. In this version, the croquettes are shaped larger—about the size of a plum—than their smaller, tapas-style counterparts and are served with a spicy sauce (I use Tabasco or Pick'a Peppa), making them ideal for a main dish. These are especially good on nights where the back deck is beckoning for the two of you to put your feet up and relax.

FOR THE CROQUETTES:

    3 tablespoons butter
    ⅓ cup flour, divided
    1 cup of milk
    1 cup finely chopped cooked turkey
    ¼ cup finely chopped sweet onions, such as
        Walla Walla or Maya
    Salt and pepper
    1 egg
    1½ cups fine dry bread crumbs, plain or seasoned
    Vegetable oil for frying

FOR THE SAUCE:

    2 tablespoons sun-dried tomato or regular
        tomato paste
    ½ teaspoon of your favorite hot sauce
    ¼ cup chopped onion
    ¼ cup chopped green bell pepper
    2 tablespoons water
    1 tablespoon dried white wine
    Salt and pepper

> ## tip
> The longer you refrigerate the croquette mixture, the easier the croquettes will be to form. This will also ensure a crispy outside and a creamy inside. The mixture can be made up to a day in advance.

1. Melt the butter in a large skillet over medium-high heat. Add 3 tablespoons of the flour and stir to form a smooth paste. Gradually add the milk, whisking constantly, until the mixture is smooth and begins to thicken, about 5 to 7 minutes.

2. Add the turkey and onion and continue to cook until the mixture begins to pull away from the sides of the pan, about 8 minutes. Remove from the heat and season with salt and pepper to taste. Place the mixture in a shallow baking dish and cover with plastic wrap. Refrigerate for at least 2 hours.

3. Beat the egg in a shallow dish with 1 teaspoon water, place the remaining flour in another shallow dish and place the bread crumbs in a third shallow dish to prepare for dredging and breading.

4. Using wet hands, shape the croquette mixture into plum-shaped meatballs. You will have between 6 and 8 croquettes, depending on their size.

5. Roll each croquette into the flour mixture to coat and shake off the excess flour. Roll them in the beaten egg and then in the bread crumbs, coating well. To fry the croquettes, heat a 1-inch depth of vegetable oil over medium-high heat and fry 3 to 4 croquettes at a time, turning frequently, until golden brown, about 5 minutes. Remove the croquettes from the skillet with a slotted spoon and drain on paper towels. Keep the croquettes warm while making the sauce.

6. To make the sauce, place all of the sauce ingredients in a blender and purée. Serve with sauce with the croquettes.

new york strip steak salad
with spinach and strawberries

A *New York Strip steak is a luxurious treat. Combined with fresh, ripe strawberries it becomes downright decadent! You'll only need one steak—and one plate. Sharing is the key goal here.*

FOR THE RUB:
>½ teaspoon paprika
>¼ teaspoon kosher salt
>½ teaspoon granulated sugar
>1 large New York strip steak (about 1 pound and 1 inch thick)

FOR THE DRESSING:
>2 tablespoons pecan, walnut, or hazelnut oil
>3 tablespoons apple cider vinegar
>2 tablespoons granulated sugar
>1 teaspoon prepared mustard
>2 tablespoons plain yogurt
>½ teaspoon cumin
>½ teaspoon onion powder
>¼ teaspoon black pepper

FOR THE SALAD:
>One 6-ounce bag of prewashed baby spinach
>1 pint strawberries, sliced
>½ cup pecan halves

1. Preheat indoor or outdoor grill to high heat. Combine the dry ingredients together for the rub. Pat the mixture onto the steak. Place the steak on the grill closest to the heat and cook for 6 minutes on each side (the steak will be medium well). Remove the meat to a warm platter and cover with a piece of aluminum foil. Allow the meat to rest as you prepare the dressing and arrange the salad.

2. Prepare the dressing by combining all of the dressing ingredients and mixing well.

3. Arrange half of the spinach on each plate. Slice the meat thinly across the grain and place half of the slices on each bed of spinach. Add half of the strawberries and pecans to each plate and drizzle the dressing over the salad.

herb-crusted rack of lamb

My husband loves this recipe. Not only is it delicious, it also makes an elegant presentation when carved at the table. The meat looks lovely served on your prettiest china, so why not set the dining room table for just the two of you, complete with elegant linens and glowing candles? Round off the effect by playing some romantic music, and serve chocolate and champagne for dessert.

1½- to 2-pound rack of lamb, trimmed
½ cup plain bread crumbs
3 tablespoons butter, melted
1 clove garlic, minced
¼ cup finely chopped onion
1 teaspoon dried parsley
½ teaspoon dried oregano

1. Preheat the oven to 350°F. Place lamb on a rack in a small roasting pan, bone side down.

2. In a small bowl combine the remaining ingredients. Press the mixture firmly onto the top of the meat.

3. Bake uncovered for 35 minutes, or until your meat thermometer registers 160°F (medium well). Remove the meat from the oven and let it rest for 5 minutes.

4. Cut the rack into individual chops before serving.

tenderloin steaks au poivre

Tenderloin is one of our favorite cuts of beef. We like to buy a nice tenderloin roast, take it home, and cut it into 1½-inch steaks ourselves, freezing a larger piece of the meat that we'll cook later as a roast. Or we cut the remaining tenderloin into chunks and use it in Beef Tips in Red Wine Tarragon Sauce (page 83). Au poivre simply means "with pepper," and freshly ground peppercorns are a must for this recipe.

Two or three 1½-inch beef tenderloin steaks (about 1¼ pounds)
1 teaspoon freshly cracked black pepper
2 tablespoons olive oil, divided
¼ cup chopped shallots
1 clove garlic, minced
1 tablespoon brandy
½ cup beef broth*

1. Rub the steaks with the pepper on all sides. Cover and refrigerate the meat for 30 minutes to an hour to let the flavor of the pepper permeate the meat.

2. In a large nonstick skillet, heat 1 tablespoon of the oil over medium-high heat. Add the steaks to the pan and cook 2 to 3 minutes on each side, or to desired degree of doneness. Remove the steaks to a warm serving platter.

3. Add the remaining oil to the pan and sauté the shallots and garlic for 1 minute, or until the garlic is lightly browned. Add the brandy and broth to the pan, scraping the browned bits from the bottom. Reduce the mixture by a third, about 8 minutes. Pour the sauce over the steaks and serve.

* Or you can use ½ cup hot water and a teaspoon of beef-flavored Better Than Bouillon.

pork sirloin tips montreal

Montreal *is such a romantic city with its unique architecture and classic style, and it was the inspiration for this dish. It can be prepared in the slow cooker or simmered slowly on the stove top—the choice is yours, and I provide directions for both. Either way it's super-easy: just combine the ingredients and forget about it for a while. Use the time you would have spent in the kitchen to be with your partner.*

1½ pounds lean pork, cut into 2-inch cubes
½ cup coarsely chopped onion
2 tablespoons tomato paste
¼ cup pure maple syrup
¼ cup vodka
1 clove garlic, minced
½ teaspoon coriander seeds, crushed
½ teaspoon paprika
½ teaspoon salt
½ teaspoon black pepper

1. For the slow cooker version, combine all ingredients in the cooker and cook on low for 6 to 7 hours, or until the pork is tender.

2. Or, on the stove top, combine all ingredients in a 3- or 4-quart Dutch oven. Cover and bring to a boil. Reduce heat to medium-low and simmer for 2 to 3 hours, or until the pork is tender.

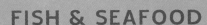

CHAPTER 6

FISH & SEAFOOD

halibut burritos *with* anaheim chile salsa

pan-seared ahi tuna *with* teriyaki glaze

tilapia *with* tropical fruit salsa

smoked salmon wraps *with* ginger dressing

seattle-style sautéed scallops *with* vodka cream sauce

lemon-glazed red snapper fillets

hazelnut-crusted salmon

nova scotia salmon *and* watercress sandwiches

crispy baked trout *with* hot tomato vinaigrette

flounder mandarinario

preserved lemons

grilled shrimp cancun *with* tomato coulis

halibut *with* lemon *and* olives

catfish *and* corn hot pot

broiled sea scallops amandine

steamed clams cadiz style

lobster linguine

halibut burritos with
anaheim chile salsa

*T**his is one of those dishes that is perfect for two grown-ups who have been playing outdoors all day. It's light and healthy and packed with flavor. Halibut is a firm, white fish, mild in flavor. It holds up well to heartier recipes such as this one. If halibut is not available, try making these burritos with fresh salmon or steelhead. Don't forget the refried beans and rice as sides!*

FOR THE BURRITOS:

> 1 tablespoon olive oil
> ¾ pound fresh halibut fillets, skin removed
> 2 large flour tortillas

FOR THE SALSA:

> ¼ cup finely chopped onion
> 1 clove garlic, minced
> ½ teaspoon lime zest
> ½ teaspoon ground cumin
> ½ cup seeded, chopped Anaheim chiles
> 2 Roma tomatoes, seeded and chopped
> Juice of one medium lime (about 2 tablespoons)
> Salt and pepper

1. Heat the oil in a large skillet over medium-high heat. Cut the halibut into 4 equal pieces and sauté in the oil, turning often, until lightly browned and the flesh begins to flake, about 5 to 8 minutes.

2. While the fish cooks, combine the salsa ingredients.

3. To serve, place half of the halibut in each tortilla and top with the salsa. Fold the tortilla burrito-style and serve.

pan-seared ahi tuna
with teriyaki glaze

*S*ushi-grade ahi tuna is expensive, but it's a wonderful indulgence for a special meal. You've spent years tending to others, so splurge on yourselves by creating this dish. As with any seafood product, always purchase your seafood from a vendor you can trust, as freshness is the key. Make this dish on the same day you purchase your fish.

¼ cup orange juice
2 tablespoons soy sauce
2 tablespoons brown sugar
2 tablespoons honey
1 clove garlic, crushed
½ teaspoon peeled and grated fresh ginger
¾ pound sushi-grade ahi (yellowfin) tuna in 2 pieces
2 tablespoons olive oil

1. Combine all ingredients except the fish and oil to make the teriyaki glaze. Set aside.

2. Heat the olive oil in a sauté pan over medium-high heat until almost smoking. Add the tuna and sear both sides of the fish, keeping the interior rare, about 2 minutes each side.

3. Preheat the broiler. Slice each piece of tuna into ¾-inch strips and place on a heatproof plate. Drizzle with the teriyaki glaze and place under the broiler for 2 to 3 minutes, or until the glaze begins to bubble. Serve immediately.

tilapia with tropical fruit salsa

Tilapia is a sweet, mild, farm-raised fish native to the Middle East. It can be found at the fish counter of most supermarkets or in the frozen food aisle. Each tilapia fillet will supply two pieces of fish per person. What we like best about this fish is that we can prepare the meal and not have the house smell fishy—tilapia has almost no odor.

FOR THE FISH:

> 2 large tilapia fillets
> 1 large egg
> 1 tablespoon water
> ¾ cup Italian-style bread crumbs
> Salt and pepper
> Olive oil for frying

FOR THE SALSA:

> ¼ cup chopped red onion
> 1 Roma tomato, seeded and chopped
> ¾ cup diced mango
> ¾ cup diced papaya
> ¼ cup diced poblano pepper or green bell pepper*
> 1 tablespoon chopped cilantro
> Juice of 1 medium lime (about 2 tablespoons)

1. Cut each fillet along its natural meridian to make 4 pieces total.

2. Beat the egg with the water in a shallow bowl. Place the bread crumbs in a second shallow bowl. Dip the tilapia pieces in the egg mixture and then coat thoroughly with the bread crumbs. Season the coated fillets with salt and pepper to taste. Place the fillets on a paper towel–lined plate to set while making the salsa.

3. To make the salsa, combine all the ingredients except the lime juice in a medium bowl. Pour the lime juice over the ingredients and toss to coat.

4. Heat 2 to 3 tablespoons of olive oil in a large nonstick skillet. When the oil is hot, add the tilapia pieces and cook for 2 minutes on each side, or until the pieces are golden brown. Do not crowd the pan.

5. Serve the tilapia immediately with the salsa.

* *Dark blackish-green poblano peppers are a very mild cousin of the jalapeño pepper, having very little "heat" in the seeds and membranes. They are only slightly hotter than a green bell pepper and give this salsa a little extra kick.*

smoked salmon wraps
with ginger dressing

*E*very once in a while my husband plays hooky from work on Friday, and we spend the day goofing off together. When our children lived at home it was our escape while they were in school. Now we play hooky because it's a fun way to spend time together. One of our favorite lunch stops is a hole-in-the-wall restaurant called Cactus YaYa in Vancouver, Washington. Their Smoked Salmon YaYa Rolls, made with their own freshly smoked salmon, inspired this recipe. Paired with ice-cold beer, this dish is heaven. It's a no-cook meal that's perfect for lunch or a light dinner.

FOR THE WRAPS:

    1 cup smoked, peppered salmon, shredded*
    1 cup shredded napa cabbage
    ½ medium onion, thinly sliced
    ½ red bell pepper, thinly sliced
    2 large (12-inch) flour tortillas

FOR THE DRESSING:

    1 tablespoon freshly grated ginger
    1 clove garlic, minced
    1 tablespoon soy sauce
    1 tablespoon sesame oil
    2 tablespoons orange juice
    1 teaspoon cider vinegar
    1 teaspoon sugar

1. Divide and arrange half of the salmon, cabbage, onion, and bell pepper along the center of each tortilla.

2. In a small bowl, combine the ingredients for the dressing. Drizzle 1 tablespoon of the dressing over the filling in each tortilla and roll each tightly around the filling.

3. Serve the rolls with the extra sauce on the side.

* *You can use almost any smoked salmon in this dish, but peppered salmon gives it just the right kick.*

seattle-style sautéed scallops
with vodka cream sauce

*F*resh scallops and Dungeness crab in a rich, creamy sauce make for a delicious, somewhat decadent dish. Serve it on its own or over hot pasta or white rice. Be sure you purchase large sea scallops—not the smaller bay scallops—for this recipe. Always cook your scallops on the same day you purchase them to guarantee freshness. We like to serve this dish in two individual ramekins and plop ourselves on pillows at the living room coffee table, just to mix things up a bit. Who says you always have to eat at the kitchen table?

8 large (about ¾ pound) sea scallops*
Salt and pepper
3 tablespoons butter
2 tablespoons finely chopped shallots
1 teaspoon all-purpose flour
½ cup heavy cream
¼ cup grated Parmesan cheese
2 tablespoons vodka
½ cup green peas (thawed if frozen)
¾ cup Dungeness crabmeat**
2 tablespoons chopped fresh Italian parsley

1. Sprinkle both sides of the scallops with salt and pepper. In a medium skillet heat the butter over medium-high heat. Add the scallops and shallots and sauté 2 minutes on each side, or until lightly browned. Remove the scallops from the pan and keep warm.

2. Sprinkle the flour into the pan and combine well with the remaining butter and shallots. Add the cream, Parmesan, and vodka to the pan, whisking to dissolve any lumps. Return the scallops to the pan and allow the sauce to thicken slightly. Add the peas and crabmeat and toss to coat, being careful to avoid breaking up the crabmeat.

3. Pour the mixture onto a serving platter and sprinkle with the parsley before serving.

* *Scallops should be cream colored or pearly rather than white—a white cast to a scallop can mean it has been treated with phosphate, a preservative. They should also have a mild, sweet odor and be somewhat firm. Soft or milky scallops indicate a previously frozen product.*

** *Freshly shelled Dungeness crabmeat is available in the fresh fish department. If it is unavailable, canned crabmeat will suffice, or you can use small, shelled, cooked shrimp instead.*

lemon-glazed red snapper fillets

Red snapper is one of the most common grocery store fish counter offerings and is inexpensive. Like any fish, it's quick to prepare and healthy to eat. If you prefer an orange or lime glaze, simply swap out the lemon—any citrus fruit will work beautifully. This dish is wonderful served with Hood River Fruited Rice (page 157).

2 snapper fillets, weighing 5 to 6 ounces each
Salt and pepper
½ cup finely chopped onion
Juice of one large lemon (about ⅓ cup)
1 teaspoon lemon zest
1 tablespoon dry white wine or sherry
1 teaspoon olive oil
1 teaspoon fresh chopped parsley

1. Preheat the oven to 375°F. Using a sharp knife, lightly score the surface of each fillet—this will help hold the glaze on the fish while cooking. Season each fillet with salt and pepper to taste.

2. In a small bowl combine the remaining ingredients except the parsley. Pour half of the mixture over the fish and bake for 10 minutes, brushing the fish often with the remaining glaze, until the fish is slightly flaky yet firm. Transfer the fish to serving plates and garnish with the fresh parsley.

hazelnut-crusted salmon

We live just a short drive from the Willamette Valley of Oregon and love to spend a leisurely day winery hopping and wine tasting. In addition to being known for its wineries and romantic bed-and-breakfast inns, this area is also known for its hazelnut orchards. Oregon growers lead the U.S. production of these tasty nuts, also called filberts or cobnuts. Hazelnuts are loaded with iron, fiber, protein, and Vitamin E. Don't be fooled by the use of honey in this recipe—it's not a sweet-tasting dish. Instead of being sweet, the honey acts as a glue agent, keeping the nuts on the fish.

> One ¾- to 1-pound salmon fillet
> Salt and pepper
> ½ cup honey
> 1 cup finely chopped raw hazelnuts
> ½ teaspoon vegetable oil

1. Preheat the oven to 350°F. Cut the salmon fillet into two pieces and season to taste with salt and pepper.

2. In a small skillet over low heat, melt the honey. Place the hazelnuts on a shallow plate.

3. Dip each piece of salmon in the honey and then in the hazelnuts, pressing the nuts firmly onto the fish. Dip only the flesh side—not the skin side—in the honey and nuts.

4. Using a paper towel, coat the inside of a small baking dish with the oil. The baking dish should be large enough to fit both fillets snugly.

5. Place the salmon fillets in the baking dish, skin side down. Bake for 15 minutes, or until the fish is cooked through and the crust has turned a golden brown.

nova scotia salmon and watercress sandwiches

While you may think of these little sandwiches as typical tea party fare, my husband and I like to eat them for supper on a warm evening or pack them into a cooler for a romantic drive along the coast. The combination of salmon and watercress is refreshing, especially when combined with a nice chilled glass of white wine and a simple salad. Use any combination of breads you have on hand. Use Nova Scotia–style salmon—sometimes just called Nova—or deli lox for these sandwiches. Other types of smoked salmon are too firm and salty for these delicate treats.

> 2 tablespoons butter, softened
> 2 tablespoons cream cheese, softened
> 4 slices fresh, soft bread such as white, whole wheat, or twelve-grain
> One 4-ounce package Nova Scotia–style smoked salmon or lox
> Salt and freshly ground black pepper
> 1 bunch watercress, cleaned and stemmed

1. For each sandwich, spread butter on one side of one piece of bread and cream cheese on one side of the other piece of bread. Place a layer of salmon on the buttered bread and season with salt and pepper to taste. Top the salmon with a layer of watercress leaves and place the slice of bread with the cream cheese face down on the sandwich.

2. Carefully remove the crusts with a serrated knife, cut each sandwich in half diagonally, and serve.

crispy baked trout with
hot tomato vinaigrette

When I was a child we didn't eat much trout—our fish selections seemed to revolve around saltwater varieties. The first time I tried trout was many years ago BC (before children) with my then-to-be-husband and his friends. Freshly caught and well prepared, it was delicious—I was hooked. This recipe is best with fresh wild trout, but fresh farm-raised trout will work as well. We still prepare trout GCFOTO (grown children finally on their own) and take turns inventing creative ways to serve it.

FOR THE TROUT:

> 2 teaspoons lemon juice
> Salt and pepper
> Two ½- to ¾-pound trout
> ¼ cup olive oil
> Flour for dredging

FOR THE VINAIGRETTE:

> 1 Roma tomato, seeded and finely chopped
> 1 tablespoon finely chopped shallots
> 1 clove garlic, finely minced
> 1 tablespoon balsamic vinegar
> 1 tablespoon dry sherry
> 1 teaspoon olive oil
> ¼ teaspoon cayenne (optional)
> Salt and pepper

1. Preheat the oven to 475°F. Sprinkle the lemon juice, salt, and pepper both inside and outside the trout.

2. Heat the oil in a large skillet over medium-high heat. Place the flour in a zipper-top bag and place the trout in the bag. Seal the bag and shake to evenly coat the fish with the flour. Remove the trout from the bag and place in the skillet with the hot oil. Brown the fish on both sides, about 5 minutes per side.

3. Place the trout in an ovenproof dish in a single layer (do not let them overlap). Place the tomato and shallots in the skillet and cook over medium-high heat until the shallots are transparent, about 5 minutes. Add the remaining ingredients, stir, and pour over the fish.

4. Bake the trout, uncovered, for 8 to 10 minutes. Serve immediately, spooning the remaining sauce from the dish over the trout.

flounder mandarinario

This dish is so simple yet so delicious. Even the most novice spouse can create this dish and serve it up in style (that's a hint for all you noncooking types). Flounder and sole can be used interchangeably and are available year-round at any market. For a change of pace, try this recipe with halibut or salmon.

¼ cup olive oil
¾ pound flounder or petrale sole fillets
Flour for dredging
Salt and pepper
One 11-ounce can mandarin orange sections, with juice*
1 teaspoon cornstarch
2 green onions, finely chopped
1 teaspoon (about a 1-inch piece) fresh ginger, peeled and minced

1. Heat the oil in a large nonstick skillet over medium heat. Dredge the flounder fillets in the flour and shake off excess. Season the fillets with salt and pepper to taste. Place the fish in the pan and sauté for 2 minutes on each side, turning carefully. The fish should flake easily with a fork but still be firm enough to hold together.

2. Drain the mandarin oranges, reserving the juice. Combine the juice with the cornstarch and pour the juice mixture in a medium saucepan. Bring to a boil slowly over medium heat, stirring constantly. When the mixture begins to thicken, add the orange sections, green onions, and ginger. Cook for 5 minutes, stirring constantly, until the sauce begins to thicken. Serve the flounder with the sauce.

* With juice, not with heavy syrup—read the can carefully before purchasing.

preserved lemons

These will keep for up to six months in the refrigerator and can be added to salads, dressings, and sauces; fish and poultry dishes; and more—anywhere you want a touch of lemon. If you have your own lemon tree, this is a wonderful way to preserve the bounty. If you don't, purchase the lemons in bags at the farmers' market.

Fresh lemons, washed and dried
Kosher salt
Glass jar with a nonreactive lid

Cut each lemon into quarters, reserving all juice. Place in the jar, sprinkling liberally with kosher salt in between the layers. Squeeze enough juice from the remaining lemons to completely cover the lemons in the jar. Cover and let the lemons cure for 3 to 4 weeks.

tip

After using the juice of fresh lemons in a recipe, bury the squeezed rind in kosher salt and keep in the fridge until you need a touch of lemon.

grilled shrimp cancun
with tomato coulis

This dish is perfect for hot summer evenings and reminds us of time spent lazily lounging on the beach in Mexico sans children and wearing not much more than a smile. Reduce the heat factor in this dish by removing the veins and seeds from the jalapeño pepper before using. For extra heat, double the amount of jalapeños. A cold Mexican beer with lime is the perfect beverage to enjoy with this dish.

FOR THE SHRIMP AND MARINADE:
>12 jumbo shrimp, shelled and deveined, with tails left on
>1 clove garlic, crushed
>Juice of ½ small lemon (about 2 tablespoons)
>½ jalapeño, finely chopped
>¼ teaspoon salt
>2 tablespoons olive oil

FOR THE COULIS:
>2 large ripe tomatoes, peeled and seeded
>1 teaspoon olive oil
>2 tablespoons minced onion
>1 clove garlic, minced
>1 tablespoon chopped fresh cilantro
>¼ teaspoon salt
>½ jalapeño, chopped

1. Place the shrimp and the marinade ingredients in a large zipper-top bag and shake well to combine. Place the bag in the refrigerator to marinate for one hour. Remove the shrimp from the marinade and reserve the marinade for brushing. Preheat indoor or outdoor grill to high heat.

2. In the meantime, place all the coulis ingredients in a blender and purée. Set aside.

3. When the grill is ready, thread 4 shrimp on each of three 8-inch metal skewers. Place the skewers on the grill with the shrimp laying flat. Grill over medium heat or coals, brushing frequently with the reserved marinade, until pink, about 2 minutes per side.

4. Serve the shrimp with the coulis on the side as a dipping sauce.

halibut with lemon and olives

You might normally think of poultry cooked in this manner—Moroccan style—but it also works well with firm fish cuts such as halibut or snapper. This recipe uses preserved lemons, which you can make yourself (page 118) or purchase at a specialty food store. The lemons are preserved in salt and must be thoroughly rinsed before using. In a pinch use a fresh lemon, although the texture will be somewhat different, and you will need to add salt to taste.

1 tablespoon olive oil
1 small yellow onion, thinly sliced
1 clove garlic, thinly sliced
¼ cup chopped preserved lemon, rinsed
¼ cup pitted green olives with pimientos
¼ cup dry white wine
¼ teaspoon white pepper
Two 5-ounce halibut fillets

> ## tip
> I like to purchase the 16-ounce bags of individually wrapped and frozen wild halibut fillets available at specialty food stores. Each bag contains four fillets. To thaw, run the fillets under cold water just before using.

1. In a medium skillet with a tight-fitting lid, heat the oil over medium-high heat.

2. Add the onion slices, sautéing until they start to caramelize around the edges, about 10 minutes. Add the garlic, lemon, olives, wine, and pepper and bring to a boil. Add the halibut, cover the skillet, and reduce the heat to a simmer. Cook for 8 to 10 minutes, or until the fish begins to flake when tested with a fork. Do not overcook.

3. To serve, place each halibut fillet on a plate and spoon the sauce over the top.

FISH & SEAFOOD

catfish and corn hot pot

Oooo-oui! *This is a delightful Acadian-style dish made with mild catfish and a ton of fresh vegetables. It's a great excuse for the two of you to head to your local farmers' market for vegetables. Bring your booty home and prepare the meal together. It's a bit messy to eat, so keep a stack of fresh napkins on hand to clean each other up.*

1 cup water
4 small red potatoes, quartered
2 ears of fresh corn, shucked and cut into 3 pieces each
¾ pound catfish pieces, cut into 3-inch chunks*
1 small onion, cut into eighths
1 small zucchini squash, cut into ¼-inch slices
¼ pound fresh whole okra**
½ medium red bell pepper, cut into 1-inch chunks
1 tablespoon butter
1 cup half-and-half
½ teaspoon prepared filé powder***
Salt and pepper

1. In a 3- or 4-quart Dutch oven combine the water, potatoes, and corn. Bring to a boil over medium-high heat, cover, and cook until the potatoes are almost tender, about 10 minutes.

2. Add the catfish, vegetables, and butter. Cover the pot and reduce the heat to medium-low. Simmer for 15 minutes, or until the potatoes are tender. Stir in the half-and-half and the filé powder. Heat through but do not allow the pot to come to a boil. Season with salt and pepper to taste and serve.

* *Catfish cheeks can also be used in this recipe.*

** *If you can't locate fresh okra, frozen whole okra will work just fine.*

*** *Filé powder is made from dried, powdered sassafras leaves and is a common seasoning and thickener in many southern and Cajun dishes.*

broiled sea scallops amandine

On a trip to Florida my husband fell for a similar dish served up at a local restaurant in Cocoa Beach. Yes, we were there to see just where I Dream of Jeannie supposedly took place—I know, it's a boomer thing, but we sure had fun! It's another terrific recipe for large sea scallops, but you can also use the smaller bay scallops. Any of your favorite nuts, including pine nuts, can be substituted for the almonds. This dish is delicious for dinner or lunch.

3 tablespoons butter, divided
8 sea scallops (about ¾ pound)
¼ cup chopped yellow onion
¼ cup dry white wine
½ cup half-and-half
Salt and pepper
½ cup grated Parmigiano-Reggiano cheese
2 tablespoons snipped fresh chives
⅓ cup sliced almonds, toasted

1. Preheat the broiler.

2. In a large ovenproof skillet heat 2 tablespoons of the butter over medium-high heat. Add the scallops and brown on both sides. Remove the scallops to a warm platter. Add the remaining butter and the onion to the pan. Cook until the onions are transparent, about 5 minutes, then add the wine and half-and-half. Cook for about 10 minutes, or until the sauce is reduced by almost half.

3. Place the scallops back in the pan. Season to taste with salt and pepper. Sprinkle the Parmigiano-Reggiano, chives, and almonds over the scallops, in that order. Broil the scallops 8 inches from the heat until the cheese melts and turns a golden brown. Serve immediately.

steamed clams cadiz style

Cadiz is a romantic, whitewashed city in the Andalusia area of Spain and is famous for flamenco and seafood. In the evening the streets are filled with couples strolling hand in hand, enjoying the cooler temperatures after a day in the searing heat of the city. In my mind, it's one of the most romantic cities on the planet. If you are unable to visit yourself, bring a little Andalusian flavor into your kitchen with this recipe. If you are unable to locate Serrano ham, prosciutto or pancetta will work nicely. Serve with a crusty bread to sop up the delicious juices.

2 tablespoons olive oil
¼ cup finely diced Serrano ham
¼ cup finely chopped onion
1 teaspoon red pepper flakes
2 cloves garlic, thinly sliced
¼ cup dry white wine
¼ cup water
2 pounds manila, rock, or littleneck clams, cleaned
2 tablespoons chopped fresh parsley

1. Heat the oil in a large skillet over medium-high heat.

2. Add the Serrano ham and the onion and cook until the ham and onions begin to brown lightly, about 3 minutes. Add the red pepper flakes and garlic and sauté until the garlic begins to brown, about 3 minutes. Add the wine and water and cook for 2 minutes. Add the clams and cover with a lid or aluminum foil. Cook for 5 to 7 minutes, or until the clams open.

3. Transfer the clams and liquid to a large serving bowl. Discard any clams that did not open. Sprinkle the parsley over the clams and serve.

lobster linguine

Dim the lights, close the curtains, and light the candles, because this is one of the ultimate romantic dinners. Turn on some mood music and dab a little cologne on those hard-to-reach spots. For the perfect musical accompaniment I recommend the soulful, sexy voice of Marvin Gaye. I can hardly wait for hubby to get home . . .

1 tablespoon olive oil
8 ounces frozen or fresh lobster meat*
1 clove garlic, crushed
¼ cup diced shallots
¼ cup dry white wine
1 cup half-and-half or heavy cream
⅓ cup grated Asiago cheese
One 9-ounce package duo linguine (half plain, half spinach)
½ teaspoon salt
2 tablespoons snipped fresh chives

tip

Crayfish and lobsters are more closely related to true lobster (having five pairs of appendages on the thorax) than the squat, spiny, and rock varieties. Those lobsters are more closely related to crabs. In fact, what you get when ordering a salad, sandwich, or pasta dish at a restaurant isn't often true lobster at all.

1. Heat the oil in a skillet over medium heat.

2. Sauté the lobster in the oil until it turns white, about 8 minutes. Reduce the heat to medium and add the garlic, shallots, and wine. Cook for 5 minutes or until bubbling. Add the half-and-half and Asiago, stirring constantly until the cheese melts and the mixture thickens, about 3 minutes. Remove the sauce from the heat and keep it warm while preparing the pasta.

3. Fill a large pot with water. Add the salt and bring to a boil. Cook the pasta until al dente according to the package directions and drain.

4. Place the cooked pasta in a large serving bowl. Pour the lobster cream sauce over the pasta and sprinkle with the chives before serving.

* *If you are unable to locate lobster meat, frozen squat lobster, spiny lobster, or rock lobster (members of the crustacean family but not true lobsters) can be used, as can crayfish meat.*

FISH & SEAFOOD

125

CHAPTER 7

VEGETABLES & POTATOES

broccolini *with* caramelized onions

sautéed chard

individual cauliflower gratins

mexican-style roast corn

broccoli- *and* cheese-stuffed potatoes

sautéed green beans *with* mushrooms

crunchy zucchini sticks

asparagus *with* balsamic vinaigrette

tangy grilled eggplant *with* feta

broiled butternut squash *with* pineapple *and* red onion

baked glazed acorn squash rings

madame deux's roasted sweet potatoes

marinated heirloom tomatoes *with* fresh basil

butter-braised celery

cabbage *with* apples *and* raisins

gingered bok choy

brussels sprouts *with* brown butter *and* hazelnuts

goat cheese mashed potatoes

roasted red potatoes parmesan

saffron potatoes *with* leeks

carrots *with* apricots

broccolini with caramelized onions

Broccolini, a cross between a Chinese kale known as gai lan (Brassica oleracea) and good ol' broccoli, is available year-round in most grocery stores. It often goes by the name of baby broccoli, although that is a misnomer, as broccolini is not truly broccoli. It can also be called asparation, its marketing name. This vegetable is often packaged in cellophane-wrapped trays containing a perfect portion for two.

1 tablespoon olive oil
1 cup thinly sliced onion
½ pound fresh broccolini, ends trimmed
½ teaspoon salt

1. Heat the olive oil in a large skillet over medium-high heat. Add the onions and sauté until golden brown and caramelized, about 10 minutes. Remove the onions from the pan, placing them in a small bowl to keep them warm. Rinse the skillet.

2. Place the broccolini in the skillet and cover with water. Add the salt and bring to a boil. Reduce heat and simmer until tender and bright green, about 3 to 5 minutes.

3. Drain the broccolini well and transfer to a serving platter. Top with the caramelized onions and serve.

sautéed chard

So simple, yet so satisfying. Did you know chard is a member of the beet family? Instead of putting its energy into growing an edible root, this variety of the Chenopodiaceae family produces lush green tops and colorful ribs. Purchase rainbow, red-ribbed, or other chard varieties at the farmers' market, as freshness is the key to mild, sweet chard instead of bitter chard that is past its prime. One standard green-grocer bundle will serve two generously.

1 large bunch chard
2 tablespoons butter
1 clove garlic, minced
Juice of one medium lemon (about ¼ cup)
Salt and pepper

1. Clean the chard thoroughly by rinsing the stalks, one at a time, under cool running water. Cut off and discard the bottom few inches of the rib. Chop the cleaned chard ribs into 2-inch chunks.

2. Melt the butter in a 3-quart Dutch oven over medium-high heat. Add the garlic and the chard pieces and sauté for 5 minutes, or until the chard begins to soften. Remove the chard to a serving dish. Drizzle with the lemon juice and season with salt and pepper to taste before serving.

individual cauliflower gratins

Cauliflower, a member of the cabbage family, is an often overlooked and highly underrated vegetable. With a single serving packing 100 percent of your daily value of vitamin C, it's great for keeping our sagging bodies healthy. In this recipe, it has been transformed into a savory side dish, and when paired with a salad it can also become a vegetarian meal in itself.

Olive oil cooking spray
1 tablespoon olive oil
1 cup cauliflower, cut into 1-inch pieces
⅓ cup chopped onion
¼ teaspoon salt
Dash of black pepper
1 tablespoon all-purpose flour
¾ cup milk
¼ cup grated Parmesan cheese
½ teaspoon dried parsley
3 tablespoons plain dry bread crumbs

> ## tip
> To make these gratins even heartier, add chopped ham or cooked, crumbled bacon to the pan when cooking the cauliflower.

1. Preheat the broiler and spray the insides of two 4-ounce ramekins or four small oven-proof dishes with the cooking spray. Place the ramekins on a baking sheet.

2. Heat the olive oil in a large skillet over medium-high heat. Add the cauliflower and onions and sauté for 4 minutes, or until they brown lightly around the edges.

3. In a small bowl combine the salt, pepper, flour, milk, Parmesan, and parsley. Whisk well to combine. Pour the mixture over the cauliflower and, stirring constantly, cook for 3 minutes, or until the mixture begins to thicken and bubble.

4. Divide the mixture between the two ramekins. Top each ramekin with half of the bread crumbs and then top the bread crumbs with a light coating of the cooking spray. Place the baking sheet with the ramekins under the broiler about 6 inches from the heat for 1 minute, or until the bread crumbs are toasted.

mexican-style roast corn

This has become one of our favorite barbecue treats during the summer months. My husband and I fell in love with this simple corn recipe on a trip to Mexico City many years ago, and we crave it during the summer months. Called elote in Spanish, it's a common street food and can be found in nearly every plaza. We enjoyed ours at the Zocalo—a truly romantic spot by night—on a warm August evening. For best results, use the freshest ears you can find: farmers' markets are the best source.

2 ears fresh sweet corn
½ cup finely grated Cotija cheese*
2 tablespoons mayonnaise
Chili powder
Salt

tip

If you don't have the barbecue going but are craving this recipe, the ears can also be roasted in a 400° oven for 10 to 15 minutes.

1. Prepare the barbecue.

2. Unwrap the corn husks and remove the silk, keeping the husks attached to the ears. Rewrap the husks and place the ears of corn on the barbecue until roasted, about 10 minutes, turning them often. The husks will char but the corn inside will not be affected.

3. Remove the husks. Place the Cotija on a small plate and smooth 1 tablespoon of mayonnaise on each ear. Roll the ears of corn in the cheese, then sprinkle each ear with chili powder and salt to taste. Serve immediately.

* If you are unable to locate this Mexican farmer cheese, substitute grated Parmesan.

broccoli- and cheese-stuffed potatoes

These are delicious served with meats; however, there's no need to turn on the oven just for one potato if you're not already roasting—just use the microwave to bake your potato. By adding diced ham or crumbled bacon to this recipe you can turn the humble potato into a meal in itself for those nights when the ease and comfort of a baked tater suits your lifestyle. In this recipe I have used one large baking potato, but you can also use two smaller ones, depending on what's in the pantry.

> 1 large baking potato
> 2 tablespoons sour cream
> ¼ cup milk
> ¼ cup grated cheddar cheese
> 3 tablespoons finely chopped onion
> 2 tablespoons finely chopped celery
> ¼ cup chopped broccoli
> Salt and pepper

1. To bake the potato in your oven, preheat the oven to 400°F. Pierce the potato with a fork and wrap in aluminum foil. Place foil-covered potato directly on the oven rack and bake for 40 to 50 minutes, or until the potatoes yield to pressure when gently squeezed.

2. To microwave, pierce the potato and place on a paper towel in the microwave. Cook on high for 6 to 8 minutes (depending on your microwave), or until tender.

3. Cut the potato in half and scoop out most of the pulp, leaving a ¼-inch shell. Combine the pulp with the sour cream and milk. Add the cheddar and vegetables and combine thoroughly. Season to taste with salt and pepper. Spoon half of the mixture into each potato shell. Serve hot—the potatoes can be reheated easily in the oven or microwave if they cool down.

sautéed green beans with mushrooms

*C*ooking for two doesn't have to be a chore. We think it's fun—especially when we use foods that our kids didn't want to eat, in this case, mushrooms. Now we can eat as many mushrooms as we want, any day of the week, and laugh all the way home from the supermarket. This recipe is easy and delicious, making it perfect for a weekday meal, but it's pretty enough for a fancier weekend meal. Fresh green beans from the farmers' market are best in this recipe, but thawed, frozen green beans will do in a pinch, as will peas.

1½ cups green beans
Dash of salt
2 tablespoons butter
½ cup sliced mushrooms
½ cup chopped onion
Salt and pepper

> ### tip
> Add even more color to this dish by using a combination of green and yellow beans, or add some diced red pepper or yellow squash.

1. In a medium saucepan, bring 2 cups of water to a boil. Add the green beans and salt. Turn the heat down to medium and cook the green beans for 5 minutes, or until they turn bright green. Do not overcook! Drain the beans and place them in a serving bowl.

2. In a medium skillet melt the butter over medium-high heat. Add the mushrooms and onion and sauté until the edges of the mushrooms begin to brown, about 8 minutes. Season with salt and pepper to taste and pour the mushrooms and onions over the green beans. Serve immediately.

crunchy zucchini sticks

If you are vegetable gardeners or live next door to one, you always have zucchini and you know you love it. Here's a tasty way to use it up. These sticks are great with a meal but also perfect for a midday snack for two—especially when paired with a couple of cold beers and a little creative flirting.

3 small (6-inch long) zucchini
Salt and pepper
2 tablespoons flour
1 egg
1 tablespoon water
½ cup unseasoned dry bread crumbs
Vegetable oil for frying

1. Cut each zucchini in half lengthwise and season to taste with salt and pepper. Dredge the zucchini sticks in the flour and shake off the excess.

2. In a shallow bowl combine the egg and the water and beat well. Place the bread crumbs in another shallow bowl.

3. Dip the zucchini strips in the egg mixture followed by the bread crumbs. Place the breaded zucchini sticks on a small baking rack and let them dry for 10 minutes.

4. Heat 1 inch of oil in a large skillet over medium-high heat. Fry the zucchini strips a few at a time in the hot oil for 3 to 4 minutes, or until golden brown on all sides. Serve immediately.

asparagus with balsamic vinaigrette

The asparagus season seems entirely too short. The tender, sweet stalks of local fresh asparagus are only available in early spring, so if I'm craving them any other time of year I resort to frozen asparagus spears. Spoil yourself by keeping a bottle of high-quality aged balsamic vinegar in your pantry. The flavor is so much more intense and dramatic when you use a truly great vinegar.

1 pound of asparagus
1 teaspoon salt
2 tablespoons minced shallot
1 tablespoon olive oil
2 tablespoons good-quality balsamic vinegar
Salt and freshly ground black pepper

1. Break off the thick bottom areas of the asparagus spears—they will snap where they need to and you need only bend them.

2. Bring a pot of water to boil over high heat and add the salt. Blanch the asparagus in the boiling water for 5 minutes. Immediately plunge the asparagus into cold water to stop the cooking process—you want them crisp-tender, not mushy or overcooked.

3. In a small jar with a tight-fitting lid, combine the shallot, olive oil, and balsamic vinegar. Shake vigorously to combine the ingredients well.

4. Arrange the asparagus on a serving platter and drizzle with the dressing. Season with salt and pepper to taste before serving.

tangy grilled eggplant with feta

If you have a grill pan or indoor electric grill, try using it instead of firing up the barbecue—I promise it will do a wonderful job. I have even used an electric panini press in a pinch! Look for globe eggplants that are firm and have no bruises. The skin should be a shiny deep purple and free of blemishes. Soft or blemished eggplants have been sitting around too long and tend to be bitter. Of course, nothing beats homegrown.

1 medium globe eggplant
Olive oil for brushing
1 tablespoon cider vinegar
1 clove garlic, minced
2 green onions, thinly sliced
Salt and pepper
⅓ cup crumbled feta cheese

> **tip**
> Refrigerate any left-overs. This dish is even better the next day after the flavors have had a chance to meld. Before serving, bring the dish back to room temperature.

1. Preheat indoor or outdoor grill to medium-high heat. Peel and slice the eggplant lengthwise into ½-inch-thick slices. Brush all sides with olive oil. Place the slices on the grill. Grill for 2 to 3 minutes on each side, or until lightly browned. Arrange the eggplant slices on a serving platter and allow them to cool to room temperature.

2. In a small bowl combine the cider vinegar, garlic, and green onions. Season the vinaigrette with salt and pepper to taste. Pour over the eggplant slices.

3. Sprinkle the feta over the eggplant and serve.

broiled butternut squash
with pineapple and red onion

This recipe goes very well with any pork dish or broiled fish. Purchasing frozen butternut squash in cubes and fresh ready-to-eat deli pineapple will turn an otherwise time-consuming recipe into a quick one. However, peeling and cubing fresh squash and having your partner slice a fresh, fragrant pineapple by hand results in a dish prepared together that will taste even better by virtue of the fresh ingredients and the time spent together in the kitchen.

> Nonstick cooking spray
> 1½ cups 1-inch cubed butternut squash
> 1 cup diced fresh pineapple
> ½ cup diced red onion
> 2 tablespoons butter or margarine, melted
> 1 tablespoon brown sugar
> ¼ teaspoon ground cinnamon
> Dash of salt

1. Preheat your broiler.

2. Spray a heatproof medium casserole dish (about 9 by 9 inches) with nonstick cooking spray. Place the squash, pineapple, and onions in the dish and broil 5 to 6 inches from the heat for 5 minutes.

3. Combine the remaining ingredients and pour over the squash mixture. Broil for an additional 5 minutes, or until the mixture is browned.

baked glazed acorn squash rings

My husband and I have often joked that there isn't a squash recipe we won't eat. We've eaten it baked, fried, mashed, stuffed, puréed, and grilled, and we love it. Acorn squash, that ubiquitous autumn market staple, was once only available in dark green, but it can now be found in golden and multicolored varieties. They all have a similar flavor and can be used interchangeably. Delicata, amber cup, and smaller butternut squashes can also be used in this recipe.

1 acorn squash
2 tablespoons butter
1 tablespoon brown sugar
1 tablespoon light corn syrup
¼ cup orange juice
¼ teaspoon cinnamon
Dash of ground cloves
Salt

1. Preheat the oven to 350°F. Slice the acorn squash into 1-inch-thick rings.

2. In a large ovenproof skillet, melt the butter over medium heat. Add the brown sugar, corn syrup, orange juice, cinnamon, and cloves. Season with salt to taste (you won't need much).

3. Place the squash rings in the pan. Place the pan in the oven and bake for 20 minutes, or until the squash is tender.

madame deux's roasted sweet potatoes

*T*he humble sweet potato is ignored most of the year and tends to only make its appearance in most homes during the winter holidays. This is a shame really, because they're delicious, available year-round, and are packed with vitamins and fiber. We call this recipe Madame Deux because it's a recipe for two, created one evening when we were feeling particularly frisky—hence the Madame part . . .

2 small sweet potatoes, peeled and quartered
1 small sweet onion, such as Walla Walla, Maya, or Vidalia
Salt and pepper
3 tablespoons butter, melted
1 tablespoon brown sugar
2 tablespoons good bourbon
⅓ cup chopped pecans

1. Preheat the oven to 400°F.

2. Place the sweet potatoes in a shallow ovenproof dish. Cut the onion into quarters and cut each quarter in half to make chunks. Season the potatoes and onions with salt and pepper to taste.

3. Combine the butter, brown sugar, and bourbon in a small bowl. Pour the butter mixture over the potatoes and onions and cover the dish tightly with aluminum foil.

4. Bake covered for 20 minutes. Remove the foil and bake for an additional 10 minutes, or until the sweet potatoes are tender and slightly caramelized.

5. In the meantime, toast the nuts in a small skillet over medium heat, stirring constantly to avoid burning. Sprinkle the nuts over the potatoes just before serving.

marinated heirloom tomatoes
with fresh basil

Visit your local farmers' market and you'll discover a huge variety of heirloom tomatoes in brilliant shades of red, orange—even a ripe green—in shapes ranging from round and pretty to pear-shaped or just plain ugly. In my opinion, ugly tomatoes tend to have the best flavor. Bring home an assortment of these pommes d'amour (love apples) for a colorful presentation.

2 cups trimmed, quartered heirloom tomatoes
3 or 4 fresh basil leaves
1 green onion
¼ cup cider vinegar
1 teaspoon olive oil
½ teaspoon brown sugar
¼ teaspoon salt
Dash of pepper
1 clove garlic, minced

1. Place the tomato wedges in a medium nonreactive bowl (such as ceramic or glass). Chop the basil leaves and add them to the tomatoes. Slice the white and light green areas of green onion thinly, discarding the darker outer part of the stalk. Add the green onion to the tomatoes.

2. Combine the remaining ingredients to make the marinade and pour over the tomatoes, basil, and green onion. Toss to coat and let stand at room temperature for one hour before serving.

butter-braised celery

Romantic couples will appreciate that celery was considered a food of love by the ancient Romans and Greeks. French cook Bernard Loiseau considered celery a "virile vegetable," and it was a favorite vegetable of Madame de Pompadour. There are several proverbs regarding celery: "Celery revitalizes old husbands," and "If women knew what celery could do for their husbands, they would go all the way to Rome to find it." A thorough search did not reveal the origins of these two proverbs, but they sound pretty good to me! Note to self: add celery to this week's shopping list. An unusual take on a common vegetable, this dish makes a delicious accompaniment to any meat dish.

½ bunch (about 6 stalks) celery
2 tablespoons unsalted butter
½ cup chicken stock
Salt and freshly ground black pepper

1. Preheat the oven to 375°F.

2. Wash and trim the celery, removing any tough strings from the stalks and discarding the tops (or save them to use in a soup). Cut the celery into 3-inch pieces.

3. Heat the butter in a large ovenproof skillet. Add the celery to the skillet and coat each piece with butter. Add the chicken stock.

4. Place the skillet in the oven and braise until the celery is tender, about 10 minutes, turning the celery often. If any liquid remains in the pan, return the pan to the stove and allow the liquid to cook off. Serve the celery hot, seasoned with salt and pepper to taste.

tip

Add 1 teaspoon chicken-flavored Better Than Bouillon to ½ cup hot water instead of opening a can of stock—no leftover liquid to worry about.

cabbage with apples and raisins

Cabbage braised with tart apples and raisins is an unusual combination, being sweet yet slightly sour, but one I'm sure you'll enjoy and make many times. Be sure to select tart cooking apples that will hold their shape while cooking—Granny Smith and Jonagold are two excellent varieties.

2 slices thick-cut bacon
⅓ cup finely chopped onion
⅓ cup thinly sliced celery
2 medium cooking apples, peeled, cored, and cut in ½-inch cubes
3 cups shredded red cabbage (about 1 small head)
½ cup chicken stock
⅓ cup dry sherry
1 teaspoon white vinegar
Salt and pepper
⅓ cup raisins

1. In a 3-quart Dutch oven over medium-high heat, cook the bacon until crispy. Remove the bacon from the pan and crumble.

2. Add the onion and celery to the pot and cook until the onions are transparent, about 5 minutes, but do not let them brown. Add the apples, cabbage, chicken stock, sherry, and vinegar. Season with salt and pepper to taste. Bring to a boil. Cover and reduce heat to a simmer and cook for 20 minutes, stirring occasionally.

3. Remove the lid and cook for an additional 10 minutes, or until most of the liquid is evaporated. Add the bacon and raisins to the pot and serve.

gingered bok choy

Bok choy is a member of the cabbage family and is a common ingredient in Asian stir-fry dishes, but it's also terrific as a vegetable side dish. Paired with ginger it takes on a delightful aroma that lingers in the mouth—it's kind of sexy. It is said that Madame du Barry, a feisty French courtesan and mistress of many French nobles during the late 1700s, used ginger to lure Louis XV into her bed. You too might want to keep a piece or two of fresh ginger on hand.

1-inch piece of ginger, peeled and thinly sliced
¼ teaspoon red pepper flakes
2 green onions
¼ cup white wine
Juice of large ½ lemon (about ¼ cup)
½ teaspoon lemon zest
1 head bok choy, or 2 to 4 heads baby bok choy
Salt

Place all of the ingredients except the bok choy and salt in a large skillet with a tight-fitting lid and bring to a boil. Reduce heat to a simmer and add the bok choy. Cover and simmer for 10 minutes, or until the thickest parts of the bok choy are tender. Season with salt to taste, and serve with the remaining sauce.

brussels sprouts with
brown butter and hazelnuts

Our entire family loves brussels sprouts. When our children were young, we would often tease that we had the only kids on the planet who liked them. As adults, they still love them, as do we. Here's one of our favorite ways to prepare them, scaled down to two delicious servings and tossed with brown butter and nuts. Watch the butter carefully as it browns, because once the process starts, it happens very quickly.

¾ pound (about 18 small) brussels sprouts
2 tablespoons butter
½ cup whole shelled hazelnuts
Salt and pepper
¼ cup grated Parmesan cheese

1. Clean the brussels sprouts by trimming off the ends and removing any yellowed or discolored outer leaves. Blanch the sprouts for 8 minutes in boiling salted water, then drain in a colander.

2. In a medium skillet, melt the butter over medium-high heat. Add the brussels sprouts and the hazelnuts and cook, stirring constantly, until the butter begins to brown, about 5 to 8 minutes.

3. Remove the pan from the heat. Season to taste with salt and pepper. Place the sprouts in a serving dish and top with the Parmesan.

goat cheese mashed potatoes

There are some of us on this planet who love mashed potatoes in any way, shape, form, or flavor. My husband is one of them! He has never met a potato he didn't like, and he likes to prepare these with me as the official "smasher." You can peel the potatoes if you prefer, but the skin is full of fiber—and we can all use the extra fiber as the years take their toll on our bodies.

2 large russet potatoes, cut into eighths
2 ounces goat cheese
2 tablespoons sour cream
2 tablespoons butter
1 tablespoon fresh, snipped chives
¼ teaspoon freshly ground black pepper

Boil the potatoes until tender in salted water. Drain. Mash the potatoes by hand with a potato masher—you want to leave some chunks. Add the remaining ingredients. Mix well to combine and serve.

roasted red potatoes parmesan

*L*ook for the smallest red potatoes you can find. Itsy-bitsy potatoes are very sweet, so they'll need little else to bring out their flavor. They'll also roast quickly and look adorable on your plate. If you have a farmers' market in your area, small fingerling potatoes are also great for this dish, especially the tiny Russian Banana and Swedish Peanut varieties.

½ pound (about 8) small new red potatoes
2 teaspoons olive oil
½ teaspoon dried rosemary, crushed
Salt and pepper
¼ cup grated Parmesan cheese

1. Preheat the oven to 400°F. Wash the potatoes and pat them dry.

2. Combine the olive oil and rosemary in a medium bowl. Toss the potatoes with the olive oil mixture to coat and place in a single layer in a shallow baking dish. Season to taste with salt and pepper.

3. Roast for 20 minutes or until the potatoes are soft, turning often. Just before serving, toss the potatoes with the Parmesan.

saffron potatoes with leeks

Saffron is the one of my favorite ingredients, despite its steep price tag. It's well worth it because it imparts a heady aroma that pairs well with starches such as rice and potatoes, which are wonderful served with roasted meats and fish. It is also said to stimulate your erogenous zones, which translates into a little extra fun, don't you think? Keep your saffron in a cool, dry place and protect it from sun exposure in an airtight container to help it retain its flavor.

2 large russet potatoes, peeled and diced into ½-inch cubes
8 saffron threads
2 tablespoons olive oil
2 cloves garlic, minced
½ cup thinly sliced leeks, white parts only
¼ teaspoon smoked paprika
2 tablespoons chopped fresh parsley

1. Bring a pot of salted water to boil. Add the potatoes and cook until barely fork-tender.

2. Remove one tablespoon of the cooking liquid from the pot and place it in a small bowl. Crush the saffron threads and add them to the liquid. Set aside. Drain the potatoes in a colander.

3. In a large nonstick skillet heat the oil over medium-high heat. Add the potatoes and fry until the potatoes are lightly browned, about 15 minutes. Add the garlic and leeks and cook for 2 minutes, or until the garlic is lightly browned and the leeks are tender. Add the reserved saffron water and the paprika. Stir to coat. Place the potatoes in a serving dish and sprinkle with the parsley just before serving.

carrots with apricots

We love to use dried fruits with sweeter vegetables such as carrots, and we always have a variety of dried fruits in our pantry. They're very convenient for boomers on the go because they're great for snacks as well as recipes such as this one or Hood River Fruited Rice (page 157). Dried peaches, cranberries, cherries, or papaya can also be used in this recipe.

½ cup dried apricots
½ cup boiling water
2 tablespoons butter
1 cup diagonally sliced ½-inch carrots
Salt
2 tablespoons honey

1. Cut each apricot in half. Soak the apricots in the water for 10 minutes and drain any excess water.

2. In a large skillet over medium-high heat, melt the butter. Add the carrots and sauté for 5 to 8 minutes, or until they are barely fork-tender. Do not overcook. Season the carrots with salt to taste.

3. Place the apricots in the pan and heat through, stirring often. Add the honey, stir to combine, and serve.

CHAPTER 8

PASTA, RICE & GRAINS

shiitake mushroom risotto

SERVES 2 TO 4

One of the great things about having an empty nest is that you can satisfy your cravings anytime you want. This is why I always keep dried shiitake mushrooms on hand in my pantry. When we're craving mushroom risotto made from scratch (we don't care for the packaged, boxed versions) we can make it right then and there. Dehydrated mushrooms are easy to use—simply soak them for a few minutes to reconstitute. Using dried mushrooms also makes it easy to use only what you need, rather than buying too much and having your mushrooms go bad. You can find dried mushrooms in the produce department in many different varieties, including chanterelles, porcini, and others—giving you plenty of opportunity to experiment. Leftover rice can be used for Risotto Balls (page 156).

1 cup dried shiitake mushrooms
1 cup warm water
One 14.5-ounce can chicken stock
2 tablespoons butter
⅓ cup chopped onion
1 cup arborio rice
¼ cup white wine
½ cup grated Parmesan cheese

1. Soak the shiitakes in the warm water in a small bowl for 20 minutes. Remove them from the water and squeeze the excess water back into the bowl, reserving the liquid. Combine the reserved mushroom liquid and the chicken stock to make 3 cups of liquid, adding a bit of water if necessary. Set aside.

2. Melt the butter in a large skillet over medium-high heat. Add the onions and shiitakes, sautéing until they are lightly browned, about 6 minutes. Add the rice, reserved mushroom chicken stock, and wine. Stir continuously until bubbling, reduce heat to medium, and cook for 15 to 20 minutes, stirring frequently, until the rice has absorbed most of the water and is tender, yet still firm to the bite. Stir in the Parmesan before serving.

risotto balls

It's tough to create a recipe for risotto that only serves two people. But you don't have to have repeats! This quick recipe will turn the remaining risotto into a snack or side dish that's just different enough to not feel like leftovers. Because the amount of leftover risotto will vary, I have not given specific quantities, but you shouldn't need them—this is almost a no-brainer.

Leftover Shiitake Mushroom Risotto (page 154) or other cooked risotto
1 egg beaten with 1 teaspoon water
Dry Italian-style bread crumbs
Vegetable oil for frying

1. Roll the leftover chilled risotto into 1-inch balls. Roll each ball in the egg mixture and then in the bread crumbs.

2. Heat 1 inch of oil in a skillet over medium-high heat. Fry the risotto balls until golden brown, remove from the skillet with a slotted spoon, and drain on paper towels. Serve immediately.

hood river fruited rice

The Hood River area of Oregon is known for its fruit and nut orchards, as well as its beautiful scenery. We like to take a leisurely drive to the area each fall and bring home our favorite fresh and dried orchard fruits. It's something we always did with the kids but now do as a couple, and it's refreshing not having anyone complaining or screaming from the back seat. Nestled at the foot of Mount Hood, the Hood River area has the ideal climate for growing orchard fruits, especially apples and pears, as well as stone fruits such as apricots and cherries. This recipe uses dried fruits rather than fresh and has a wonderful aroma and a fruity flavor that's not too sweet. It's also quick to prepare, making a lovely presentation that is perfect for using up leftover rice. This recipe pairs well with the Turkey Schnitzel with Mustard Sauce (page 76) and a nice Oregon chardonnay.

¼ cup diced dried cherries
¼ cup diced dried apricots
¼ cup diced dried apples or pears
1 cup hot water
2 tablespoons butter or margarine
½ cup chopped celery
¼ cup diced red onion
1 cup cooked white rice
¼ cup chopped hazelnuts or pecans, toasted

tip

To toast nuts, put them in a hot skillet and stir until lightly browned. Nuts contain oils and toast quickly, so use caution to avoid burning them.

1. Combine the fruit and water in a small bowl and soak for 5 minutes. Drain the fruit.

2. Melt the butter in a large skillet. Add the celery and onions, and cook until the onions are transparent, about 5 minutes. Add the fruit and the rice and heat through. Sprinkle with the toasted hazelnuts before serving.

PASTA, RICE & GRAINS

pasta primavera

A *quintessential springtime treat and a cross between a meal and a salad, pasta primavera is one of our warm-weather favorites. Any fresh seasonal vegetables can be used instead of—or in addition to—the ones listed here. There's a lot of slicing and dicing involved, which makes this a perfect recipe to be prepared by two . . . for two.*

4 ounces angel hair pasta
2 tablespoons olive oil, divided
⅓ cup broccoli flowerets
⅓ cup sliced zucchini
⅓ cup sliced yellow squash
⅓ cup sliced yellow bell pepper
⅓ cup frozen peas, thawed
⅓ cup thinly sliced carrots
⅓ cup snow pea pods, strings removed
⅓ cup thinly sliced green onions
6 cherry tomatoes
¼ cup pine nuts, toasted
1 tablespoon fresh chopped parsley
1 tablespoon fresh chopped basil
Salt and pepper
⅓ cup grated Parmesan cheese

1. Cook the pasta in a pot of boiling salted water until al dente according to package directions. Place the pasta in a colander and rinse with cold water to stop the cooking process (allowing the pasta to cool naturally will result in mushy pasta).

2. In a large skillet heat one tablespoon of the olive oil over medium-high heat. Add all the vegetables except the green onions and tomatoes and cook for 5 minutes, or until the carrots begin to soften slightly. Do not overcook. Remove the pan from the stove, place the vegetables in a bowl, and chill for one hour.

3. In a large serving bowl combine the pasta, chilled vegetables, green onions, and tomatoes. Season to taste with salt and pepper. Sprinkle the pine nuts, Parmesan, parsley, and basil over the vegetables and drizzle with the remaining olive oil. Toss to combine, and serve.

rice salad andaluz

Hot, lazy days call for fun in the sun for two and require easy recipes—especially those that you can fix and forget until you're both ready to eat. Crispy gazpacho-inspired vegetables and rice combined with a simple dressing make this a refreshing summer salad. You can turn it into a meal by adding a bit of leftover ham or chicken to it. It sure beats heating up the kitchen (to cook, that is).

1 cup cooked rice, cooled (leftover rice is perfect)
¼ cup chopped red bell pepper
½ cup peeled, cubed cucumber
½ cup cherry or grape tomatoes, halved
¼ cup sliced black olives
¼ cup thinly sliced green onions
1 clove garlic, minced
2 tablespoons olive oil
1½ teaspoons red wine vinegar
¼ teaspoon salt
1 tablespoon chopped fresh parsley

1. In a serving bowl toss together the rice, bell pepper, cucumber, tomatoes, olives, and green onions.

2. To make the dressing combine the remaining ingredients. Mix well and pour over the rice mixture. Chill for at least one hour before serving.

savory baked barley

Barley has been used as a food source for millennia and is the fourth-largest grain crop after wheat, rice, and corn. Traces of this cereal grain are still found in ancient tombs in Egypt, Asia, and all over Europe, and it made its way to the Americas with the explorers. Barley makes a wonderful and unusual side dish, has a chewy yet pleasing consistency, and is an excellent source of fiber, vitamins, and protein. Serve as a side dish with meats, or substitute vegetable stock for the beef stock and pair the barley with a salad for a savory vegan lunch.

2 tablespoons butter or margarine
½ cup chopped onion
¼ cup chopped celery
½ cup chopped green bell pepper
½ cup finely chopped carrots
½ cup pearl barley
1½ cups hot beef stock
Salt and freshly ground black pepper

1. Preheat the oven to 350°F.

2. Melt the butter in a medium ovenproof pan with a well-fitting lid. Add the onion, celery, bell pepper, and carrots. Sauté until the onions are transparent, about 5 minutes. Add the barley and the beef stock. Season to taste with salt and pepper. Cover the pot and bake for 45 minutes, or until the barley is tender and the liquid has been absorbed.

black beans and rice with serrano ham

Beans have always been one of our favorite comfort foods. Here, we combine black beans and rice with one of my favorite ingredients, Spanish Serrano ham, making this dish almost a meal in itself. We like to serve this with roast pork or chicken, or to skip the ham and create a semi-vegetarian meal. You can also use red beans in this recipe.

½ cup chicken stock
1 cup water
¾ cup rice
1 tablespoon olive oil
½ cup chopped onion
⅓ cup chopped green bell pepper
2 cloves garlic, thinly sliced
1 cup dried black beans, rinsed
1 tablespoon white vinegar
1 teaspoon cumin seed, crushed
1 small bay leaf
1 cup diced Serrano ham

1. Place the chicken stock and water in a medium saucepan and bring to a boil over medium-high heat. Add the rice and cover. Turn the heat down to medium and cook the rice until it is soft and the liquid has been absorbed.

2. Meanwhile, in a large saucepan with a fitted lid heat the olive oil over medium-high heat. Add the onion, bell pepper, and garlic, stirring constantly and cooking until the onions are transparent, about 5 minutes. Add the beans and enough water to cover. Pour in the vinegar and add the cumin seed, bay leaf, and ham. Bring the mixture to a boil. Cover, reduce the heat to medium, and cook for 1 to 2 hours, or until the beans are tender. Check the bean pot often and add water if the mixture begins to cook dry before the beans are tender.

3. When the beans are tender, remove the bay leaf from the bean pot. Stir the rice into the beans and serve.

curried lentils

In this recipe, I have used a slow cooker to slowly simmer the lentils. The aroma is wonderful to return home to after a busy boomer day at work or play. The lentils will be very soft, similar to a dal, so serve this dish over a bed of hot rice with a side salad.

¾ cup dried lentils
2 cups water
One 14.5-ounce can vegetable stock
1 medium tomato, seeded and chopped
1 medium potato, peeled and cut in 1-inch cubes
⅓ cup thinly sliced carrots
⅓ cup thinly sliced celery
⅓ cup chopped onion
¼ cup raisins
1 clove garlic, minced
1 tablespoon lime juice
1½ teaspoons curry powder
¼ teaspoon salt

Add all ingredients to your slow cooker and stir to fully combine. Cover and cook on low for 6 to 8 hours, or until the lentils are tender.

couscous with sautéed vegetables

Plain couscous is available in the rice and beans aisle of most major supermarkets—but don't confuse it with the preseasoned, mass-produced, boxed variety. If you are lucky enough to find Israeli couscous, which has larger grains than regular couscous, it can be used as well. Any leftovers can be easily reheated in the microwave. We've been known to serve the leftovers cold as a salad, drizzled with vinaigrette.

1 cup chicken stock
1 cup plain couscous
1 tablespoon olive oil
⅓ cup chopped onion
⅓ cup thinly sliced carrots
⅓ cup thinly sliced celery
¾ cup butternut squash, cut into 1-inch cubes
½ cup halved baby pattypan squash
⅓ cup green beans, cut into 1-inch pieces
Salt and pepper
1 teaspoon dried parsley

1. Bring the chicken stock to a boil in a small saucepan. Add the couscous, stir, and remove from the heat. When the couscous has absorbed the liquid, after about 7 minutes, fluff it with a fork and keep warm.

2. In the meantime, heat the oil in a large skillet over medium-high heat. Add the vegetables and sauté until the carrots are slightly tender, about 10 minutes. Do not overcook. Season with salt and pepper to taste.

3. Arrange the couscous on a serving platter to form a well. Place the vegetables inside the well of couscous and sprinkle with the parsley before serving.

creamy bowties with crab and cheddar

*T*his isn't your kids' macaroni and cheese! Instead, this is comfort food taken to the next level and is just for grown-ups. It makes a great lunch or dinner entrée that is sure to please you both. Serve this dish with a crisp green salad and a nice glass of white wine and settle in for the night.

1½ cups bowtie pasta
2 tablespoons butter
¼ cup chopped shallots
1 tablespoon all-purpose flour
1 cup milk
½ cup frozen peas, thawed
1 cup shredded medium cheddar cheese
1 cup lump crabmeat
Salt and pepper
2 tablespoons plain dry bread crumbs
Cooking spray

1. Preheat the broiler.

2. Cook the pasta in boiling salted water until al dente according to package directions. Drain and keep warm.

3. Melt the butter in a large skillet over medium heat. Add the shallots and sauté until transparent, about 5 minutes. Stir in the flour and combine well, removing any lumps. Add the milk and whisk until the mixture begins to thicken, about 3 minutes. Add the cheddar and whisk until melted and smooth, about 4 minutes. Add the peas and heat through.

4. Remove the pan from the heat and add the crabmeat, combining without breaking up the lumps. Check the seasonings and add salt and pepper to taste if desired.

5. Pour the mixture into a small baking dish and top with the bread crumbs. Give the bread crumbs a shot of the cooking spray. Place under the broiler, no closer than 6 inches to the heat, for 1 to 2 minutes, or until the bread crumbs are browned, and serve.

orzo with greens and garlic

Orzo is a small rice-shaped pasta available just about everywhere. Acini di pepe—or any other small pasta shape—can also be used in this dish. Spinach or other leafy greens can be swapped for the chard, depending on availability. In a pinch, a box of frozen spinach or chard will work just fine as well. This dish can be prepared very quickly, in just the time it takes to boil water, cook the pasta (which cooks quickly due to its small size), and sauté the remaining ingredients. It makes a nice side dish for meats and can also stand on its own as a lunch item.

1 cup orzo
1 tablespoon olive oil
¼ cup chopped shallots
2 cups chopped greens such as chard or spinach
2 cloves garlic, minced
4 slices of bacon, fried crisp and crumbled
Salt and pepper

1. Cook the orzo in boiling salted water until tender and drain in a colander.

2. Heat the oil in a large skillet over medium-high heat. Add the shallots and cook for 2 minutes, or until shallots are transparent. Add the greens and the garlic, sautéing until the greens begin to wilt, about 2 minutes. Do not overcook. Remove the pan from the heat and stir the cooked orzo and bacon into the greens mixture. Season with salt and pepper to taste.

no-fuss lasagne

Here's a dilemma: the hubby absolutely adores lasagne; however, making it these days is not only a chore, but the recipe makes enough to feed an entire army. The solution? Ditch the wide lasagna noodles and pare down the ingredients to a more manageable amount. This recipe is related closely enough that it will take care of both of your cravings yet provide just enough lasagne to avoid weeks of leftovers.

2 cups lasagnotti pasta*
½ pound lean ground beef or pork
1 tablespoon olive oil
½ cup chopped onion
1 clove garlic, minced
1 cup sliced mushrooms
One 14.5-ounce can diced tomatoes in juice
½ cup ricotta cheese
1 teaspoon herbes de Provence
1 cup grated Parmesan cheese

1. Preheat the broiler.

2. Cook the pasta in boiling, salted water until al dente according to package directions. Drain in a colander and place the pasta in a large heatproof bowl.

3. In a medium skillet over medium-high heat, brown the ground beef. Drain any fat. Add the olive oil and onion to the skillet. Cook until the onions are transparent, about 5 minutes, and add the garlic, mushrooms, and tomatoes with their juice. Cook for 5 minutes to heat through. Add the ricotta and the herbes de Provence, stirring to mix well.

4. Combine the sauce with the pasta in the large bowl, mixing thoroughly. Place the mixture in an ovenproof casserole and sprinkle with the Parmesan. Broil the casserole 6 inches from the heat until the cheese is melted and serve.

* *Lasagnotti can be difficult to find. A suitable substitute is regular lasagna noodles broken into 2-inch chunks, or you can use campanelli or farfalle.*

rotini with prosciutto and goat cheese

There's just something about goat cheese and prosciutto that screams romance. Maybe it's because *where the items originated or the landscape and language. Maybe it's just because it tastes so rich an. decadent. Regardless of the reason, this dish rates high on the romance meter.*

1½ cups rotini
1 tablespoon olive oil
⅓ cup chopped shallots
⅓ cup diced prosciutto*
2 tablespoons julienne sun-dried tomatoes
⅓ cup fresh fava beans or edamame
½ cup chicken stock
1 tablespoon finely chopped fresh basil
½ cup crumbled goat cheese

1. Cook the rotini in boiling salted water until al dente according to package directions. Drain in a colander and keep the pasta warm.

2. In a large skillet heat the olive oil over medium heat. Add the shallots and cook until they become transparent, about 5 minutes. Add the prosciutto, sundried tomatoes, beans, and chicken stock. Cook for 5 minutes, or until the mixture begins to thicken. Add the pasta to the pan and toss to combine. Toss in the basil and goat cheese just before serving.

* *Prediced prosciutto is usually found in the deli department, near the presliced packaged prosciutto. Pancetta or thinly sliced bacon, cooked and chopped, can be substituted if desired.*

tijuana rice

As a small child living in Southern California, I visited Tijuana often with my mother. Her parents lived there (Spaniards by birth, they immigrated to Mexico in the 1940s after the Spanish Civil War) and owned a chain of liquor stores and art galleries. This was back when Tijuana was still a quaint town with little more going for it than food, art, and culture—certainly not the sprawling city it is today. My favorite part of every visit to Tijuana, other than seeing my grandparents and picking fresh figs from their backyard tree, was helping in the kitchen. This recipe, scaled down for two, was inspired by those visits and is terrific served with Grilled Skirt Steak (page 81) and a side of guacamole. Unfortunately, Tijuana is no longer a sleepy little town, and my husband has never really been much of a fan of the area, due to an "incident" while in college (one of the joys of being a boomer youth). Apparently, Tijuana jails really were as bad as that old song written and sung by the Kingston Trio.

1 tablespoon olive oil
½ cup finely chopped onion
¼ cup finely diced green bell pepper or poblano chile
1 clove garlic, minced
1½ cups water
1 tablespoon (or 1 cube) Caldo de Tomate con Sabor de Pollo*
¼ teaspoon ground cumin
¾ cup long-grain white rice

Heat the oil in a medium saucepan and cook the onions until lightly browned, about 10 minutes. Add the bell pepper and garlic and sauté for 1 minute. Add the water, Caldo de Tomate, and cumin. Stir until dissolved and bring to a boil. Add the rice. Cover, reduce heat, and simmer for 15 minutes, or until the rice is tender.

* *Caldo de Tomate con Sabor de Pollo is a tomato bouillon with a chicken base (see page 5). If you don't keep this ingredient on hand, you can substitute 1 teaspoon tomato paste and use 1 cup chicken stock instead of water.*

PASTA, RICE & GRAINS

CHAPTER 9

BREADS

strawberry amaretto scones

fluffy dinner rolls

sweet potato *and* spice quick bread

savory sun-dried tomato drop biscuits

rustic flatbread

pizza margherita

herbed breadsticks

oatmeal cranberry tea loaf

peanut butter *and* raisin banana bread

strawberry amaretto scones

MAKES 8 SMALL OR 6 LARGE SCONES

*N*o one can resist the indulgence of breakfast in bed—especially when presented with these delectable scones, fresh from the oven. The combination of dried strawberries and amaretto liqueur gives these scones a decadent, sexy aroma. You don't need an electric mixer to prepare this recipe, so it can be made quietly enough for a delightful surprise.

1⅓ cups all-purpose flour
⅓ cup granulated sugar
1 teaspoon baking powder
⅛ teaspoon salt
½ cup (1 stick) unsalted butter, chilled and diced
1 tablespoon amaretto liqueur or almond extract
½ cup heavy cream
⅓ cup dried strawberries, cut into ¼-inch
   (raisin-sized) pieces

1. Preheat the oven to 400°F.

2. Combine the first four ingredients in a medium mixing bowl. Cut in the butter with two knives or a pastry blender (or pulse using your food processor) until the mixture resembles coarse cornmeal. Add the amaretto and cream to the flour mixture. Add the strawberry pieces and mix just until combined.

3. Pat out the dough onto a piece of waxed paper and roll it until it is 1 inch thick. To make 8 smaller scones, shape the dough into a 6- by 6-inch square and cut into quarters to make 4 squares. Cut each square in half to make a triangle. For larger scones, shape the dough into a 9- by 3-inch rectangle and cut the rectangle into 3 squares. Cut each square in half to make triangles.

4. Place the scones 2 inches apart on a baking sheet lined with a silicone baking sheet or parchment paper. Bake 10 to 15 minutes, or until lightly browned on top. Serve warm with butter and jam.

tip

You can substitute any other dried fruit for the strawberries or use other flavored liqueurs. For example, dried cranberries go well with orange-flavored liqueurs; dried peaches or apricots complement a cinnamon liqueur; and raisins, currants, or sultanas go well with rum.

fluffy dinner rolls

MAKES 6 ROLLS

*N*othing smells better or will attract your mate to the kitchen faster than freshly baked bread. Create your own come-hither aroma using this simple small-batch recipe for fluffy white rolls. You may make them by hand or enlist the help of your bread machine. Customize them with add-ins such as herbs or shredded cheese.

> 1½ teaspoons active dry yeast
> 1¼ cups warm water
> 3 cups all-purpose flour
> 1 teaspoon salt
> 1 teaspoon sugar
> 1 tablespoon olive oil

1. In a small bowl, dissolve the yeast in the warm water. In a large bowl, combine the flour, salt, and sugar. Add the olive oil to the yeast mixture and add the yeast mixture to the flour mixture. Mix well.

2. Turn the dough out onto a lightly floured surface and knead until smooth, about 5 minutes. Place the dough in an oiled bowl and turn the dough over so that all sides are oiled. Cover and let rise in a warm place until doubled, about 1½ hours.

3. Grease a 9- by 9-inch greased baking pan. Punch down the dough and divide it into 6 equal pieces. Roll each piece into a ball and place the balls in the pan. Cover and let rise until doubled, about 1 hour.

4. Preheat the oven to 375°F. Place the pan in the oven and bake for 15 minutes, or until the rolls are golden brown on the top.

sweet potato and spice quick bread

MAKES 1 SMALL LOAF OR 6 MEDIUM MUFFINS

*T*his is a terrific recipe for using up leftover mashed sweet potatoes or pumpkin. I've given directions for both a small loaf and a six-pack of muffins. It makes a wonderful breakfast, snack, or picnic take-along.

1½ cups all-purpose flour
1 teaspoon baking powder
¼ teaspoon salt
½ teaspoon ground cinnamon
¼ teaspoon ground cloves
¼ teaspoon ground ginger
1 large egg
2 tablespoons milk
¾ cup cooked mashed sweet potatoes
½ cup chopped walnuts or pecans

tip

If you'd like, add in ⅓ cup of your favorite fruit chunks—raisins, chopped apples, or dried fruit—just before baking for a change of pace.

1. Preheat the oven to 350°F. Grease the bottom of an 8- by 8- by 2½-inch loaf pan or 6 wells in a standard cupcake pan.

2. In a large bowl combine the flour, baking powder, salt, cinnamon, cloves, and ginger. In a medium bowl beat the egg with the milk; add the mashed sweet potatoes and stir to blend well. Add the wet ingredients to the dry ingredients until the mixture is just moistened—do not overstir. Fold in the walnuts.

3. Pour the batter into the pan or wells. Bake the loaf pan for 30 to 45 minutes and the muffin pan for 25 minutes, or until a toothpick inserted in the center of the loaf or muffins comes out clean. Cool pans on a wire rack for 15 to 20 minutes, turn out the bread or muffins, and continue cooling on the wire rack.

savory sun-dried tomato drop biscuits

I know of a few boomers who have resorted to using boxed biscuit mix instead of from-scratch biscuits simply because their favorite recipe makes a huge batch. Throw away the box and try this recipe instead. These hand-shaped biscuits are a cinch to make and tend to be lighter and fluffier than rolled biscuits. Just be sure to handle the dough as little as possible. You can easily get creative with this recipe by substituting other chopped vegetables for the sun-dried tomatoes and onions, and you can use other cheeses as well.

1 cup all-purpose flour
1 teaspoon baking powder
½ teaspoon salt
¼ teaspoon baking soda
¼ cup (½ stick) butter, chilled and cut into ¼-inch chunks
⅓ cup milk
¼ cup sour cream
¼ cup finely diced sun-dried tomatoes
1 clove garlic, diced
¼ cup shredded medium or sharp cheddar cheese
1 tablespoon chopped onion
¼ teaspoon dried basil

1. Preheat the oven to 425°F.

2. Combine the first four ingredients in a medium bowl. Cut in the butter with two knives or a pastry blender (or pulse using your food processor) until the mixture resembles coarse cornmeal.

3. Add the remaining ingredients and stir to evenly distribute throughout the dough. Roll the dough into four equal-sized balls and flatten each ball so that it is 1 inch thick. Place the dough balls on a nonstick baking sheet or one that has been lined with a silicone baking sheet or parchment paper. Bake for 15 minutes or until golden brown. Serve warm with plenty of butter.

rustic flatbread

MAKES EIGHT 6-INCH PIECES

*T*his is one of our favorite Saturday afternoon pastimes—making flatbread. When they're fresh and still steaming from the griddle, it's hard not to sample these delicious rounds before serving! We like them almost naked—drizzled with a bit of good olive oil and sprinkled with coarse salt. Flatbread is quicker and easier to make than regular raised bread, and it goes well with everything from dips and salads to main courses, stews, and soups. Best of all, the ingredients in this recipe are common pantry items—flour, water, yeast, salt, sugar, and oil are the only requirements. While this flatbread can easily be made on top of the stove using a griddle or large frying pan, I do recommend using an electric griddle or pan. A high temperature is necessary, and an electric pan makes it easier to control the heat by taking the guesswork out of it; just set the knob to the desired temperature. Use the same dough for Pizza Margherita (page 184) or Herbed Breadsticks (page 185)!

> 2 cups all-purpose flour
> 1 teaspoon active dry yeast
> ¾ cup warm water
> ½ teaspoon salt
> ½ teaspoon granulated sugar
> 1 tablespoon olive oil, plus additional for oiling the bowl and griddle

1. Sift the flour into the bowl of a stand mixer fitted with a dough hook.

2. In a small bowl, dissolve the yeast in the warm water. Add the salt, sugar, and olive oil to the yeast mixture and stir to combine. While mixing at medium speed, drizzle the yeast mixture into the flour until combined. Knead by hand or machine for an additional 8 to 10 minutes, or until the dough becomes smooth and satiny.

3. Oil a medium mixing bowl with additional olive oil. Remove the dough from the mixer and shape it into a ball. Place the ball in the oiled bowl and then turn the ball over so that all sides of the dough are coated with the oil. Cover the bowl with plastic wrap and allow the dough to rise until doubled, about 1½ hours.

4. Punch down the dough and turn out onto a floured surface. Knead by hand for 2 minutes. Divide the dough into 8 pieces and shape each piece into a smooth ball. Roll out each ball into a 6-inch round circle and place the rounds on a baking sheet covered with a towel. Let the rounds of dough rest for 10 minutes.

5. Heat a large, flat griddle (electric or stovetop) to 475°F. Lightly oil the griddle by using a paper towel dipped in olive oil. Place the rounds of dough on the griddle, spacing them at least 2 inches apart. Cook on one side for 2 minutes, or until the centers begin to puff slightly. Turn each round over and cook for an additional 2 minutes on the other side. Keep the rounds warm until serving by wrapping them in aluminum foil.

pizza margherita

A *classic recipe pared down for two using the same dough as for the Rustic Flatbread (pages 182–83). It's handy having such a versatile dough in your recipe repertoire. Use the first half of the batch of dough to make the flatbread, then use the second half to make these wonderful pizzas. The dough will keep for a day or two in the fridge after you punch it down after the first rise.*

½ batch Rustic Flatbread dough (pages 182–83)
2 ripe Roma tomatoes, thinly sliced
⅓ cup coarsely chopped fresh basil
1½ cups freshly grated mozzarella
Olive oil for drizzling

1. Prepare the dough as directed in the Rustic Flatbread recipe through to the first rise. Punch down the dough and divide it into 4 equal pieces. Roll out each piece into a 10-inch circle. Let rest for 15 minutes.

2. Preheat the oven to 475°F.

3. Arrange ¼ of the Roma tomato slices and basil on each round of dough. Sprinkle ¼ of the mozzarella on top of each pizza and drizzle with olive oil.

4. Bake the pizzas, two at a time, for 8 to 10 minutes, or until the crust is lightly browned.

herbed breadsticks

*A*nother use for the dough recipe from Rustic Flatbread (pages 182–83). I like to use a combination of crushed cumin (crushed by hand with a mortar and pestle to preserve chunkiness) and garlic powder on my breadsticks, but you can use your own favorite herb combination.

½ batch Rustic Flatbread dough (pages 182–83)
1 egg white, beaten
Assorted dried herbs
Kosher salt

1. Prepare the dough as directed in the Rustic Flatbread recipe through to the first rise. Preheat the oven to 400°F.

2. Punch down the dough and divide it into 16 equal pieces. Roll each piece into a stick measuring 10 inches in length. Brush each stick with the egg white, roll in the herbs, and sprinkle with the kosher salt.

3. Place the sticks 1 inch apart on a nonstick baking sheet or one that has been lined with a silicone baking sheet or parchment paper.

4. Bake for 10 to 12 minutes, or until golden brown. The breadsticks can be kept refrigerated in a sealed container for several days.

oatmeal cranberry tea loaf

MAKES 1 SMALL LOAF

Moist and fruity, this bread is delicious used for turkey or chicken sandwiches. It's also nice toasted or fresh from the oven with a pat of butter. Because it makes a small loaf, you'll be able to enjoy it before it goes stale—a dream come true in a house of two.

1½ cups flour
1 cup quick-cooking rolled oats
1 teaspoon baking powder
½ teaspoon salt
½ cup dried cranberries
1 egg, beaten with 1 teaspoon water
¼ cup honey
⅔ cup milk

1. Preheat the oven to 350°F. Grease and flour an 8- by 8- by 2½-inch loaf pan.

2. In a large mixing bowl combine the first five ingredients and mix well. Add the egg mixture, honey, and milk. Stir to combine—the mixture will be lumpy.

3. Pour the batter into the loaf pan and bake for 50 to 60 minutes, or until a toothpick inserted in the center of the loaf comes out clean. Cool on a wire rack, turn out loaf, and continue cooling on the wire rack.

peanut butter and
raisin banana bread

MAKES 1 SMALL LOAF

Banana bread has always been a favorite treat. In this recipe it is combined with another favorite, peanut butter, creating a rich, moist bread you'll make again and again. It's great for breakfast or a snack. Toast the leftovers and serve in bed; a few well-placed crumbs will give you an excuse to move a bit closer to your bedmate later that night.

1½ cups all-purpose flour
2 teaspoons baking soda
½ teaspoon salt
1 cup granulated sugar
⅓ cup (5 tablespoons plus 1 teaspoon) butter or margarine, softened
¾ cup crunchy peanut butter
2 large eggs, lightly beaten
1 cup (about 2 medium) ripe mashed bananas
⅓ cup raisins

1. Preheat the oven to 350°F. Grease and flour an 8- by 8- by 2½-inch loaf pan.

2. In a medium bowl combine the flour, baking soda, and salt. In a large bowl cream the sugar and butter together. Beat in the peanut butter and the eggs. Add the bananas and raisins and stir well to combine.

3. Stir the dry ingredients into the peanut butter mixture a little at a time, beating well after each addition. Pour into the loaf pan and bake for 50 to 60 minutes, or until a toothpick inserted in the center of the loaf comes out clean. Cool on a wire rack, turn out loaf, and continue cooling on the wire rack.

CHAPTER 10

DESSERTS & BEVERAGES

choux . . . for two

rich *and* easy chocolate fondue

cinnamon rice pudding

spiced apples *with* ice cream

blueberry walnut bread pudding

creamy fruit clafoutis

tuscan-style cantaloupe *with* honey yogurt dressing

rum *and* raisin cakes

racy raspberry rum tea

strawberry smoothie parfaits

coffeetinis

choux . . . for two

MAKES 8 SMALL PUFFS

Romance is in the air when you serve these delicate (yet easy) puffs of pastry for breakfast in bed! This recipe was inspired by the wonderful choux puffs served at St. Honoré Boulangerie in the trendy Pearl District of Portland, Oregon. Pronounced "shoo," these puffs are wonderful for Valentine's Day, an anniversary, or another special occasion, served with a piping hot cup of coffee or tea. The centers are hollow—like puffs of air—making them perfect receptacles for your favorite jam or fruit preserves. While eight puffs may seem like a large quantity for two, their airiness makes them light, and they'll definitely disappear quickly.

This recipe is simple, whips up and bakes quickly, and does not require any special pans or ingredients. In fact, everything you need is already in your pantry—right down to your favorite fruit preserves or jam. The trick to making a batch this small is in lightly beating the egg before adding half of it at a time to the dough.

> ¼ cup water
> 2 tablespoons unsalted butter
> ¼ teaspoon pure vanilla extract
> 1 teaspoon granulated sugar
> ¼ cup all-purpose flour
> 1 egg, lightly beaten, at room temperature
> Sprinkling sugar or coarse raw sugar
> Jam or fruit preserves

1. Preheat the oven to 375°F. Line a medium baking sheet with a silicone baking sheet or or parchment paper.

2. Combine the water, butter, vanilla and granulated sugar in a saucepan and bring to a boil. Remove the pan from the heat and, using a wooden spoon, stir in the flour, stirring until the mixture forms a ball and pulls away from the sides of the pan.

3. Beat in the egg, one half at a time, until the dough is smooth. Drop the dough by teaspoonfuls onto the lined baking sheet, spacing them at least 2 inches apart to allow for expansion during baking. Sprinkle each patch of dough liberally with sprinkling sugar.

4. Bake for 20 minutes, or until golden brown. For best results, do not open the oven while the puffs are baking. If you must peek, use the window.

5. Serve warm with your favorite jam.

rich and easy chocolate fondue

Chocolate is still the ultimate passion-inducing food. Take advantage of its come-hither properties by creating this dessert quickly while the mood is right. As long as you have a bag of chocolate chips and a can of sweetened condensed milk in your pantry, you have a decadent, naughty dessert! Serve this fondue style with cubes of cake or with fresh fruits such as strawberries, melon cubes, and banana chunks, and you'll be revered forever as a cooking god or goddess.

> One 14-ounce can sweetened condensed milk (not evaporated milk)
> 2 cups semisweet or milk chocolate chips

In a small saucepan heat the milk over medium heat until it just starts to bubble around the edges—do not let the milk come to a boil. Remove the pan from the heat and add the chocolate chips, stirring constantly until they melt. Enjoy immediately.

cinnamon rice pudding

Creamy and satisfying, rice pudding is the ultimate cold-weather comfort food, especially good when you're cuddled up on the couch watching old movies. It's also a nice way to use up leftover rice and can be flavored with your favorite dried fruits. We've been known to slice a banana over our bowls and eat this for breakfast on occasion. When it's just the two of you, who's going to know you're eating dessert for breakfast?

1 cup cooked white or brown rice
2 cups milk
½ teaspoon ground cinnamon
1 tablespoon butter
⅓ cup granulated sugar
¼ teaspoon orange or lemon extract
3 tablespoons half-and-half
2 egg whites

1. In a large saucepan combine the rice, milk, cinnamon, and butter. Simmer for 10 minutes, or until half of the liquid has been absorbed. Stir in the sugar, orange extract, and the half-and-half.

2. In a small bowl beat the egg whites until soft peaks form. Gently fold the egg whites into the rice mixture and serve warm.

spiced apples with ice cream

*S*erve this mixture warm over vanilla ice cream—or alone. Either way it will satisfy your spouse's sweet tooth without loading up on too many fats. This is also good spooned onto hot oatmeal in the morning. Don't you just love recipes that have multiple uses?

½ teaspoon butter
1 large Granny Smith apple, peeled, cored, and sliced thinly
¼ cup corn syrup
½ teaspoon ground cinnamon
¼ teaspoon ground cloves
¼ cup chopped pecans
Vanilla ice cream

Melt the butter in a medium skillet over medium-high heat. Add the apple slices and cook until they begin to brown lightly around the edges, about 5 minutes. Reduce the heat to low and add the remaining ingredients. Heat through and serve over a scoop of vanilla ice cream.

blueberry walnut bread pudding

This recipe is perfect for using up the last few slices of bread that have gone a bit stale. Crusts can be trimmed or left on the bread, depending on your preference. The addition of blueberries and walnuts makes this pudding perfect not only for dessert, but also for a special breakfast or brunch. It is delicious served warm or at room temperature. I also like to use this recipe with other fresh seasonal fruits such as apples, ripe pears, or cherries.

¼ cup (½ stick) butter or margarine, softened
½ cup granulated sugar
2 large eggs
½ teaspoon pure vanilla extract
¾ cups bread cubes, crusts removed (about 2 slices)
¾ cup fresh or frozen blueberries
¼ cup chopped walnuts
Powdered sugar for dusting

1. Preheat the oven to 325°F. Butter two individual serving dishes or two 8-ounce ramekins.

2. In the bowl of an electric mixer, or by hand, cream the butter and sugar until fluffy. Add the eggs, one at a time, beating thoroughly after each addition. Add the vanilla and mix to combine all ingredients. Remove the bowl from the mixer.

3. Add the bread cubes, blueberries*, and walnuts to the mixture, pushing the bread and nuts into the bowl using a rubber spatula until they are well coated.

4. Place the serving dishes on a baking sheet without allowing them to touch each other (to allow for better heat circulation). Fill each dish within ¼ inch of the top.

5. Place the baking sheet with filled dishes in the oven and bake for 20 to 25 minutes, or until a knife inserted in the centers comes out clean.

6. Dust with powdered sugar before serving.

* *If using frozen blueberries, add them to the serving dishes after the batter has been poured to avoid discoloring the batter with the blueberry juices.*

creamy fruit clafoutis

MAKES TWO 6-OUNCE OR FOUR 3-OUNCE SERVINGS

*T*his is an easy custard to prepare and it makes a lovely dessert for a romantic evening for two. We've also been known to eat it for breakfast on a hot summer morning or whenever we're feeling the urge for something sweet but not heavy. The size of your ramekins determines the serving size here.

> 1 cup fresh cherries (pitted and halved), or strawberries (hulled and halved)
> 1 tablespoon butter
> ⅓ cup granulated sugar, divided
> 1 large egg
> 2 tablespoons flour
> ¾ cup milk

1. Preheat the oven to 400°F. Butter two 6-ounce or four 3-ounce ramekins.

2. Sprinkle the fruit with 2 tablespoons of the granulated sugar. Place the fruit at the bottom of the ramekins.

3. Combine the remaining sugar with the butter, egg, flour, and milk, beating by hand or with an electric mixer for 2 minutes, or until smooth. Pour the batter over the fruit.

4. Bake for 10 minutes. Reduce the heat to 325°F and bake an additional 5 to 8 minutes, or until a knife inserted in the centers comes out clean. Larger ramekins may need a few extra minutes to set the centers.

tuscan-style cantaloupe with honey yogurt dressing

Fruit has been a traditional dessert in other countries for centuries. It's healthy and refreshing, and tastes so good. If you can't locate a Tuscan-style cantaloupe, a standard melon will work just as well but will definitely not be quite as sweet. You can always add a touch more honey, Honey.

> 1 ripe Dulcinea Tuscan-style cantaloupe*
> ½ cup plain yogurt
> ¼ cup honey
> 2 tablespoons chopped fresh mint leaves

1. Slice the melon into ¼-inch slices and remove the skin. Arrange the slices on a platter.

2. Combine the remaining ingredients and whisk well to eliminate any lumps. Pour the dressing over the melon and serve.

* Dulcinea is a branded European-style melon that is quickly appearing in grocery store produce departments. Unlike other cantaloupes, this melon is clearly ridged. To determine ripeness, take a look at the grooves of the melon. Green grooves indicate a melon that is sweet but firm, and not quite ripe. Light-colored grooves indicate a melon that is soft in texture and extra sweet—meaning it's perfectly ripe.

rum and raisin cakes

MAKES TWO 6-OUNCE OR FOUR 3-OUNCE CAKES

*T*his cake is dense, moist, and flavored with dark rum, making it decadent and delightfully sinful. Serve with whipped topping or a scoop of ice cream if desired. If you do not have mini baba au rhum tins, mini cake pans, ramekins, or a muffin pan will work just as well. The number of cakes will depend on the type and size of your pans, but typically you will have two 6-ounce cakes or four muffin-sized cakes.

¼ cup boiling water
2 teaspoons dark rum
3 tablespoons raisins or currants
3 tablespoons melted butter
1 egg, beaten
⅓ cup granulated sugar
½ cup all-purpose flour
¼ teaspoon baking soda
1 tablespoon unsweetened cocoa powder
¼ teaspoon ground cloves
¼ cup chopped walnuts

1. Preheat the oven to 350°F. Butter and flour the insides of two large or four small baba au rhum tins.

2. In a heatproof small bowl combine the boiling water, rum, and raisins. Add the melted butter to the rum mixture and let cool for 10 minutes. Beat the egg into the mixture.

3. In a large bowl combine the remaining ingredients. Add the rum mixture to the dry ingredients, adding a quarter at a time and beating well between each addition. Pour the batter into the prepared tins.

4. Place the tins on a baking sheet and bake for 30 to 40 minutes, or until a toothpick inserted in the centers comes out clean. Cool pans on a wire rack for 5 minutes. Turn out cakes and continue cooling on the wire rack.

racy raspberry rum tea

*D*elicious on a hot summer evening, this love potion is easy enough to double, triple, or make by the pitcherful (it just depends on how much energy you have, right?). The combination of berries and rum is fabulous as it is, but adding strong tea perks up your energy level and gives your evening a little extra kick. Thaw the raspberries in the refrigerator just to the point where you can separate the berries—do not thaw completely because they'll become too mushy.

    1 shot white rum
    1 shot vodka
    1 shot crushed frozen raspberries with juice
    1 cup strong black tea
    Crushed ice

Combine all ingredients in a shaker. Pour over crushed ice in an old-fashioned or highball glass.

strawberry smoothie parfaits

If you're going to have dessert, it may as well be semihealthy, which is why we use yogurt with the gelatin and fruit. It adds creaminess without adding too much fat in the form of whipped cream. We still use a dollop of whipped cream—just to keep up appearances. My husband loves these parfaits.

One 3-ounce package strawberry gelatin
1 cup boiling water
½ cup cold water
One 6-ounce container strawberry yogurt
1 cup sliced fresh strawberries

1. In a heatproof bowl combine the gelatin with the boiling water. Stir well to dissolve. Add the cold water and the yogurt. Mix well to combine the ingredients and eliminate any yogurt lumps.

2. Chill for 20 minutes. Stir in the strawberries and spoon into dessert dishes or glasses. Chill for an additional 30 minutes and serve.

coffeetinis

*H*ere I give you two very seductive, liquid desserts in martini glasses—how sexy! You decide which way you want to go: dark and delightful or smooth and sexy. Either way you can't go wrong. Making these tasty gems will ensure that the sizzle will never fizzle.

VERSION ONE: DARK AND DELIGHTFUL

1 shot strong espresso
1 shot Kahlúa or other coffee-flavored liqueur
1 shot vanilla vodka
1 cup ice

Combine all ingredients in a beverage shaker. Shake well, strain, and serve in a martini glass.

VERSION TWO: SMOOTH AND CREAMY

Sugar
1 shot strong espresso
1 shot Irish cream liqueur
1 shot vanilla vodka
1 shot half-and-half

Wet the rim of a martini glass and dip in sugar to coat the rim. Combine all ingredients in a beverage shaker. Shake well, strain, and serve in the sugared martini glass.

APPENDIX

BABY BOOMER RESOURCES

The following Web sites contain useful information for baby boomers and empty nesters.

AARP (AMERICAN ASSOCIATION OF RETIRED PERSONS)
www.aarp.org

You knew you'd be one eventually. Now it's your turn to check out the AARP. The AARP publishes a terrific magazine; offers member discounts for insurance, travel, and more; and features information on consumer issues, social security, and finances. A very useful site.

AGING HIPSTERS
www.aginghipsters.com

A fun site featuring everything about baby boom popular culture, from music to humor and everything in between, plus forums and blogs. This is a great place to visit while surfing the Net.

THE BOOMER PROJECT
www.boomerproject.com/resources.asp

A terrific source of research materials and statistics about the baby boom generation, though still a work in progress. Worth a visit or two.

BOOMERS INTERNATIONAL
http://boomersint.org

This Web site contains good articles and resources for boomers, especially in the areas of health, finance, and retirement.

RESOURCES FOR SPECIALTY FOOD PRODUCTS AND SUPPLIES

AMBASSADOR SEAFOODS
www.ambassadorseafoods.com/lang.html
120 NW 165th St. Road, Suite 104, Miami, FL 33169
800-365-2016 or 305-940-9133

A source for frozen squat lobster as well as tilapia and mahimahi.

COOKING.COM

www.cooking.com

2850 Ocean Park Boulevard, Suite 310, Santa Monica, CA 90405

310-450-3270 or 800-663-8810

Cooking.com carries 1-pound loaf pans (8.5 x 4.5 x 2.75 inches), as well as ¼-pound pans and mini pans.

IGOURMET.COM

www.igourmet.com

508 Delaware Avenue, West Pittston, PA 18643

877-446-8763

A terrific resource for specialty products such as salted capers, quality anchovy paste, and fine wines and cheeses. Spoil yourself.

PACIFIC SEAFOOD GROUP

www.pacseafood.com

16797 SE 130th Avenue, Clackamas, OR 97015

503-905-4500

A source for quality frozen seafood products, including wild halibut, several varieties of salmon, mahimahi, shellfish, and spiny lobster. The site also features a nice collection of seafood recipes.

SUR LA TABLE

www.surlatable.com

5701 Sixth Avenue S, Suite 486, Seattle, WA 98108

206-613-6000 or 800-243-0852

Now that it's just the two of you, indulge your passion for specialty kitchenware, gadgets, and gourmet food items.

INDEX

ABOUT THE AUTHOR

Cheryl Fall is a baby boomer, empty nester, and author of twelve how-to books and over 2,000 published how-to articles. Her work has been featured in *Woman's World*, *Family Circle*, *Country Living*, and many others. She is also the host, creative director, and co-founder of the PBS Plus television series entitled *The Creative Life with Cheryl Fall*. This nationally distributed, magazine-style show features interesting information on cooking, crafts, gardening, and home décor.

Cheryl is a member of the IACP (International Association of Culinary Professionals), the USPCA (United States Personal Chef Association), and the AG (Authors Guild). She has also written articles for the online food styling magazine Foodesigns.com.

She and her husband reside in Washington State.